TRIGGER™
The voice of mental health

The**inspirational**series™
Overcoming adversity and thriving

Within The White Lines
How The Beautiful Game Saved My Life
BY RUTH FOX

We are proud to introduce The**inspirational**series™. Part of the Trigger family of innovative mental health books, The**inspirational**series™ tells the stories of the people who have battled and beaten mental health issues. For more information visit: www.triggerpublishing.com

THE AUTHO

D0301189

Ruth Fox is a mental health campaigner, author, footballer and public speaker. She was diagnosed with depression at age 14 and has since faced a difficult battle with the illness. She reached her lowest point in November 2017, when she was admitted into hospital following self-harm and suicidal thoughts.

Ruth painstakingly rebuilt her life and has now found her purpose in helping others. Her goal is to have a positive impact on as many people as possible, especially in the sporting world, by emphasising the importance of mental health training. She is a proud ambassador and advisor for The Shaw Mind Foundation and Mental Health FA.

First published in Great Britain 2018 by Trigger

Trigger is a trading style of Shaw Callaghan Ltd & Shaw Callaghan 23 USA, INC.

The Foundation Centre

Navigation House, 48 Millgate, Newark

Nottinghamshire NG24 4TS UK

www.triggerpublishing.com

Copyright © Ruth Fox 2018

British Library Cataloguing in Publication Data

A CIP catalogue record for this book is available upon request
from the British Library

ISBN: 978-1-912478-60-6

This book is also available in the following e-Book and Audio formats:

MOBI: 978-1-912478-63-7
EPUB: 978-1-912478-61-3
PDF: 978-1-912478-62-0
AUDIO: 978-1-912478-64-4

Ruth Fox has asserted her right under the Copyright,
Design and Patents Act 1988 to be identified as the author of this work

Cover design and typeset by Fusion Graphic Design Ltd

Printed and bound in Great Britain by Clays Ltd, Elcograf S.p.A.

Paper from responsible sources

TRIGGER™

The voice of mental health

www.triggerpublishing.com

Thank you for purchasing this book.
You are making an incredible difference.

Proceeds from all Trigger books go directly to
The Shaw Mind Foundation, a global charity that focuses
entirely on mental health. To find out more about
The Shaw Mind Foundation visit,
www.shawmindfoundation.org

MISSION STATEMENT

Our goal is to make help and support available for every
single person in society, from all walks of life.
We will never stop offering hope. These are our promises.

Trigger and The Shaw Mind Foundation

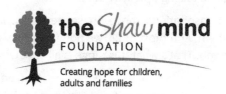

the Shaw mind
FOUNDATION

Creating hope for children,
adults and families

A NOTE FROM THE SERIES EDITOR

The Inspirational range from Trigger brings you genuine stories about our authors' experiences with mental health problems.

Some of the stories in our Inspirational range will move you to tears. Some will make you laugh. Some will make you feel angry, or surprised, or uplifted. Hopefully they will all change the way you see mental health problems.

These are stories we can all relate to and engage with. Stories of people experiencing mental health difficulties and finding their own ways to overcome them with dignity, humour, perseverance and spirit.

Ruth's story gives a no-holds-barred account of how depression brought her sporting career to an abrupt halt, and how her love of sport then helped her to overcome her difficulties and become a mental health campaigner. Her story describes how people with depression can sometimes be unaware of any clear causes of the illness, and that depression can affect anyone – regardless of social class or background. It shows the power of support networks and the importance of connecting and talking openly with others.

This is our Inspirational range. These are our stories. We hope you enjoy them. And most of all, we hope that they will educate and inspire you. That's what this range is all about.

Lauren Callaghan,
Co-founder and Lead Consultant Psychologist at Trigger

To Mr Donoghue

Disclaimer: Some names and identifying details have been changed to protect the privacy of individuals.

Trigger Warning: This book contains references to suicide, suicidal ideation, suicidal thoughts, self-harm and overdosing.

FOREWORD

Ruth Fox popped up on my Twitter feed and immediately stood out. Mental health is a focal point in my life, and depression is a subject very close to my heart, so I noticed this special, brave young woman reaching out. I had a read into her story and realised that she was a fellow athlete sharing her struggles and ultimately doing her best to fight them.

Ruth asked me to write the foreword for this amazing book, and I was overwhelmed and touched that she asked me. We are about to meet each other very soon, and I'm looking forward to meeting someone so inspiring.

Ruth shows me and so many others that even the young can have a leading role in bringing this topic to the forefront. It ruins so many lives. One of the key elements to overcoming the battle is speaking out and educating others. Ruth shows that life circumstances can affect anyone's mind, whether it's an injury, missing a loved one or anything else.

I've read this book and relate to certain things within it. I realise that what Ruth is doing at 19 years old is courageous. She is educating those who don't know what it feels like to feel so low at times.

I think she's a wonderful young lady and I support her with all my heart. This book is BRAVE. Ruth is trying to lead while also trying to face her own issues. That's special enough in itself.

I wish her nothing but love.

Leon McKenzie

PROLOGUE

The 18-year-old girl's blonde hair was mangled and wet with tears. Her eyes were red, her cheeks puffy. She was sitting alone in her bedroom, in total darkness – just like she had done dozens of times before. Only this time, she knew it would be the last time.

A heavy silence hung in the air. Her body seemed limp and lifeless, as though it had given up on her. She used to be an aspiring footballer and strong athlete, but it had all come to nothing. Depression had beaten this once strong, vibrant woman. She'd finally reached her pain threshold and could no longer hang on.

The girl was broken, bruised, defeated, and desperate. Life had pushed her further and further into a dark corner – one from which she couldn't escape. Intrusive thoughts ran through her head, overshadowing anything positive that had ever happened to her. The image of her jumping in front of a train rekindled in her mind every time she closed her eyes. The pain at the moment of collision would be worth it if it would end her ongoing suffering. She saw no future ahead of her. There was just blackness.

She wrote her suicide letter that night. The paper was sodden with tears and the ink ran. But that didn't matter. Nothing did anymore. No words would ever be enough to describe her pain.

She planned to take her life the following day. This was the only way she thought she could escape from her demons.

This girl was me. This is how I got there.

But, more importantly, this is how I got out ...

INTRODUCTION

When people look at me they see a bubbly, confident, and outgoing young woman. They see a determined and ambitious person. I smile at people as I walk past, I laugh uncontrollably at the most random things, I push myself ridiculously hard in the gym, and I don't cry in front of people. The word "depressed" wouldn't really cross anyone's mind. That's because of the image and depiction of this illness.

Depression isn't always tears and suicide letters (although both of these do appear in my story). It affects each of its victims differently, and it is not a one-size-fits-all illness. For me, just one of the 300 million people who suffer worldwide (according to the World Health Organization (WHO)), it's an unexplainable black cloud which envelopes every part of my life. It's like being thrown into the middle of a vast ocean and realising that I no longer know how to swim. It's like I'm suffocating from the inside, growing weaker and weaker. For me depression means feeling completely alone and isolated, despite having many people fighting my corner. It's knowing every single day that giving up is the easier option, but I choose to struggle on despite constant exhaustion.

You could have all the friends in the world, but no one is in your head with you and no one can fight those demons on your behalf. Depression is part of my day-to-day life. When I'm feeling bad, I put on a brave face. I smile and I laugh on tough days, but that doesn't mean that everything's okay. Depression's invisibility cloak is one of its most devastating qualities.

A smile can hold in so much pain. Often the longer someone has to wear a mask, the more convincing it is. And the harder it is to take off.

According to the WHO, close to 800,000 people die from suicide worldwide every year. However, what this shocking figure doesn't measure is the devastating number of people that each suicide directly impacts. The most heartbreaking suicide stories are the ones where family members had no idea that their loved ones were struggling in the first place. Only afterwards do they think about what could've been done to stop it – when it's too late.

However, it can be preventable with the right intervention. Far too frequently we hear of young people and adults being denied the support that they desperately need because they're considered not ill enough. We hear of people with anorexia who are not deemed at a low enough weight and people with depression who are not enough of a danger to themselves. This results in crisis before any support is offered. The system is flawed in my opinion. Having had first-hand experience of both Child and Adolescent Mental Health Services (CAMHS) and adult mental health services, I believe that there is room for a lot of improvement.

Every person you meet is fighting their own battle. They just encounter different demons and they fight them in different ways. My own story is hard-hitting and difficult to read, but unfortunately not uncommon. Nothing in these pages is more than I've had to live through.

It is easy to close the door on the past, and it's tempting to move on and try to forget. But I want to be real and honest, which leaves me entirely exposed. If my story can touch just one person out there then I feel that my job is done and my experiences haven't gone to waste.

I want to make an impact on someone. I truly hope that person is you.

CHAPTER 1

FOX IN THE BOX

As a child I was a vibrant, energetic, sporty, and bright young girl with an infectious laugh and a cute, blonde bob. That is a world away from the suicidal, depressed teenager I became, unable to see a future ahead of her. I never imagined that I'd go through such an ordeal, or that I'd ever be associated with the word "depression". I certainly never imagined that depression would nearly end my life. It came as such a shock to me and everyone who knew me.

I was blessed with an incredible upbringing. I was safe and I was happy. I was naturally academic and always gave 100% to everything I did. I enjoyed learning when I was growing up, so school was never a chore for me. I could pick things up quickly and wouldn't give up on something until I had mastered it. I began to enjoy being top of the class in a lot of things. I put in a lot of work and effort, always making sure homework was done in time. I got no less than 9 out of 10 in spelling tests and I kept myself organised. In junior school I was awarded "silver leaves" which were given out to students who had either done a kind act, achieved highly in a test, or won races on Sports Day. I accumulated near enough 150 silver leaves during my time at Pixmore Junior School. I was Scout of the Year, played Cinderella in my school Christmas production, and was form captain for my house every year.

I was never arrogant but I was never satisfied. I enjoyed achieving, but I took little time to pat myself on the back before setting my sights on the next challenge or task. Despite coming from a family of high achievers (my dad is a dentist, one of his sisters is a barrister, and his other sister is a HIV/AIDS consultant at the forefront of her field of research), I didn't ever feel any pressure to succeed from anyone else. I wanted to (and still want to) reach my full potential in everything I did, and if that meant being the top of my class, so be it.

In my mind, the only competition was beating the person I was the day before. It didn't matter how I compared with other people – I didn't give a damn. I just wanted to be my best.

I looked forward to school parents' evenings (weird, I know) where teachers would acknowledge my hard work throughout the year. Most of my teachers used the word "conscientious", and despite not having a clue what it meant, I was grateful and smiled at them. People respected that I worked hard every day, that my success was not just handed to me on a plate.

I was a fairly quiet kid. I had friends around me and I had a laugh with them, but I lacked confidence and my self-esteem was never sky-high. I still doubted myself, even when all around me was going well. I never felt that I was good enough or particularly worthy of praise.

I would always focus on the negatives. If a teacher said, 'Ruth needs to answer questions a bit more in lessons,' I would work on that over the next term. There was always a 'but' when I received praise, because if the teachers didn't have one, I added one myself.

'Ruth, you got 92% in that test!' my parents would point out gleefully.

'But it wasn't 100%,' I would reply.

While some students got reports saying "must try harder", mine often read "Ruth has proven to be an excellent student, whose level of understanding is first rate." Mum and Dad always congratulated me, but congratulations weren't necessary. I didn't need others to say, "well done!" for me to continue working hard. It was in my nature. Deep down, I had a desire to succeed.

I'm the second of two children, and I'm four years younger than my sister, Becky. Becky has always been someone who lights up a room; she's everybody's friend and a truly wonderful person. We had an unbreakable bond, a shared sense of humour, a common understanding, and a lifelong friendship. Every waking moment I had was spent by her side. We'd spend hours playing in the woods at the bottom of the garden. We'd always end up in stitches watching Hot Fuzz or *Shaun of the Dead* – the Simon Pegg Hollywood films – even though we knew all the scenes off by heart. We would spend a lot of our free time bouncing on the trampoline in our garden, even in torrential rain (because this was somehow so much more fun, though slightly precarious at times). We didn't have a care in the world and we just enjoyed every moment of our untroubled childhoods.

Soon we realised that we were developing into very different individuals. I had a compelling drive inside me to win from an early age, whereas Becky was very much a people-person, with an admirably caring side to her. I could never have wished for anyone else to be my sister and I was proud to call her that every single day. I always beamed with pride whenever Becky introduced me to her friends. *That's my big sister,* I would think to myself.

When I was about seven years old, I'd go with my dad to the nearby field and throw a cricket ball, hit a tennis ball, or kick a football. We'd do this every Saturday morning while Becky was playing the cello in the orchestra, before picking up some 'Saturday sweets' with our pocket money. As the weeks and months progressed, I became obsessed with football. At such a tender age, I fell in love with the beautiful game. I loved the skills, the shots, the tackles, the intensity, the unpredictability, the excitement, the tension, and the spirit.

Every week Dad and I would play 1v1, with trees or jumpers acting as goalposts. It got to the stage where I would thrash my dad 10–0 most weekends. I didn't know then that not many girls played football because I wasn't ever exposed to that idea. When I watched football on TV with my dad, I didn't find it odd that they were all men. I just saw it as football, and enjoyed it for the beautiful game, not for their genders. It wasn't until I asked my dad if I could join a team that I realised the options to join a side just for girls were incredibly sparse, if not impossible. There were no girl's teams at all in my area, so I joined a boy's side called HC Cougars. I really didn't mind as I just wanted to play football. The game excited me and filled me with a bubbling joy that nothing had ever done before. It made no odds whether I was playing with boys, full-grown men, or girls. I just wanted to play.

I started off playing as goalkeeper because my teammates were sceptical as to whether I could play football. Very quickly I realised that people had this "girls can't play football" attitude.

Although no one made comments about me being a girl to my face, opposition teams always saw me as a weak link. 'You just got tackled by a girl!' was a phrase I heard shouted out most weeks. And even my own teammates would refuse to pass me the ball when I first started playing, which frustrated me. Why should being a girl make any difference whatsoever? I could still play football. I was better than a lot of the boys, although they struggled to accept that.

But I soon began to prove them wrong. I would play half a game as goalkeeper, and the other half wherever they put me on the pitch. It could've been left wing, striker, or centre midfield – I didn't mind. I just did the job, worked hard, and enjoyed it immensely.

Centre midfield was the position I loved the most. I was the pivot player, dictating play, pinging balls wide, putting in strong tackles ('You just got tackled by a girl ... again!'), and scoring goals. The more I played the more I proved myself, so the less I had to play in goal and the more freedom I was given out on the pitch.

I was named Manager's Player of the Season for all four years that I was there. I beamed with pride when my name was called out at the End of Season Awards. It was nice to feel recognised. Despite a lot of people doubting my ability because of my gender, my feet always did the talking, and I was rewarded for it. Winning was always a shock, but I was becoming an integral part of the team and my teammates couldn't hide from that.

Deep down I was always on the hunt to play for a female side. I wanted to see what the standard was like and I wanted to see where my football could take me. I was also aware that when I turned 14 I would have to make the move by law anyway. In 2010, the Fox "clan" moved from Letchworth – the world's first Garden City – to Langford, a small village just off the A1 in the countryside of central Bedfordshire. This was when I was given my opportunity to join a girls' team.

One Saturday, as usual, my dad and I were kicking a ball around at the field down from our house. The chairman of the local club, Langford Girls, approached us. He was walking his dog and had stood from afar, watching us for a while. Lots of dads and their kids were spending their Saturday in the same way as we were. He walked over and told me that I looked like a decent player. He also told me that the village girls' team was always looking for new players. I was thrilled.

I thrived in the environment at Langford Girls Football Club. I felt confident and just loved having a ball at my feet. I was made captain in my second season, and I grew into the leadership role on the pitch. I became a completely different person when

I crossed the white lines of the football pitch every Saturday morning. Football was my way of communicating.

I'm sure thousands of other people up and down the country feel the same way. That's what the beautiful game does to people.

At Pixmore Junior School I was given the nickname "Fox in the Box" by my PE teacher, Mr Willard, who was someone who really inspired me to hone in on this passion of mine. In one season I scored 35 goals for the school's first ever girls football team. I was in the same class as MK Dons starlet, Hugo Logan, and have fond memories of playing football on the playground with him and the other boys. He has since signed a professional contract for the club. I represented my county for football, hockey, and cross-country, and also had England Rounders trials. I trialled for Watford, Luton, and MK Dons, turning down opportunities to be involved in their development set-ups because the distances were long and the travelling took up a lot of time.

Despite growing into an all-round athlete, I was always driven to improve and progress as a footballer particularly.

By the end of the 2012 / 2013 season, having spent three years carrying my team on my shoulders, I was in desperate need of a new challenge. I was 13 years old and I was always the player who gave my all, putting my body on the line every single game. I scored goals and I prevented the oppositions' goals from going in. I was also the only player who would spend a lot of my free time with a ball at the local field, trying out new skills, practising free kicks, and doing sprints. I even researched the best diets for athletes and started to refine what I was eating so I would perform at my best.

I was primarily playing as centre-back to strengthen the defence for the team, but really I was naturally a centre midfielder. Centre midfielders have a lot more freedom to run with the ball, take on players and attack. They make and score goals. Centre-backs play in the centre of the defence; I was put there because I was one of the few who could head the ball and maintain the shape of the back line. I felt like I needed to use my creativity, footballing brain, and attacking nature. I was being restricted in centre-back and it wasn't helping me develop as a footballer. I needed to be surrounded by teammates who would push me every training session, and I needed to be in an environment where I had to fight to be involved in the starting XI every week. It was easy for me at the level I was playing at. I was well within my comfort zone, a place where too many people spend too much of their lives. In order for me to grow and develop as an athlete and as a footballer, I needed to make that move.

I kept an eye out for alternative clubs, clubs whose attitudes and mindsets were to win and succeed – not just to play socially or for fun. As a result, I ended up joining the current league leaders and county cup winners, Kempston Colts U15s, who I had always looked forward to playing against. They were the challenge that I craved. Telling my managers that I was moving on at the end of the season was difficult because I'd enjoyed my time at Langford Girls immensely. But they acknowledged that I was destined for bigger things, and it was time to push on and reach my full potential.

Kempston welcomed me with open arms. They respected me as a player, having played against me several times. After just one trial with them I immediately felt at home, and in my first tournament playing for them that summer, I won my first piece of silverware – the Milton Keynes City Tournament Cup. I loved winning, and so did my teammates. The technical ability in this group was like nothing I'd come across before, and I was honoured to be part of it.

I don't remember having a single worry in the world during this time. I just enjoyed the little things and tried to reach my full potential in everything I did.

The move from junior school to secondary school is one that many find daunting and scary, but I was actually fine with it. Change is always hard to deal with, especially for young children, who can be scared of new teachers, homework, exams, and not making friends. But emotionally, I embraced it all. I have always loved a challenge and this change was no different. I was certainly ready to move on from junior school; they'd done a great job in developing me as a person and I wanted to go on and make them proud. My best friend and I were the only ones who went to private schools (different ones to each other) in our year group, so we did a little bit differently to our peers. That wasn't a problem for us, though. I started attending secondary school in 2010. It was the school that my dad had gone to for Sixth Form and was ranked in the top 100 independent schools in England. I thrived on this challenge. A lot of my new classmates had come from the prep school, but I didn't let that stop me from pushing myself to work hard. Ultimately it paid off and I became one of the highest achieving students in my year group. I also did my best to support my friends when they had a bad day or when they were challenged with life at home. I stood by their sides, listened, and tried to be there for them.

It would have been very difficult to predict that the next few months would turn out like they did, but it's just a reminder to appreciate and be grateful for the current moment and what you have. You never know how long it will last.

CHAPTER 2

THE FIRST HIT

No one can know for sure how a single event will affect a particular individual. Something that seems like water off a duck's back to one person can be a real life-changing, emotional rollercoaster for another. So, although this might seem like nothing to a lot of people, my whole world quickly crumbled before my eyes when my sister left for Aston University in October 2013 to study psychology and sociology.

As she'd progressed through Sixth Form, Becky had begun to find herself and grow in confidence. She'd made loads of friends and it meant that she slowly, subconsciously, moved away from me.

One of my favourite parts of the day had always been snack time after school. We'd get home and have a glass of squash, a chocolate brioche, or some pitta bread and hummus, and from this moment onwards we'd spend the rest of the evening together. But as we got older, Becky started partying at weekends, staying round at her friends' houses, sleeping in late when hungover, and studying late into the evening on school nights. I was also out most evenings at hockey or football training, and I had my own steady pile of homework to do. I just accepted it at the time. I understood that this was a pivotal period in her life – she had A Levels to complete, so she would soon be off to university. This is what she wanted, so it was what I also wanted. But during the summer I bugged her all the time to come and play badminton with me or play with the hosepipe while we washed the car. It didn't work, though, because Dad would tell me to leave her to her studying. There were a few subjects she had to work really hard on in order to get the grades she needed.

In hindsight, I wish I'd been more selfish now. I wish I'd pushed her to take five minutes away from her work, just so we could spend a few more moments together in a carefree world. It's only now that I truly recognise that these were the best days of my life.

I had never been unable to cope with any of life's challenges before, so I didn't expect this event to be any different. And yet, during the school half term in October 2013 – after Becky had left for uni – I had uncontrollable urges to cry all day, every day. I didn't know why. It felt like something was very wrong. At the time, I had no idea that it was triggered by Becky leaving home.

Sport was, and still is, my subconscious way of dealing with any kind of stress, and this is what I turned to. I also started to look at ways to improve my football performance beyond training on the pitch. I was fitter than anyone I played against – faster, stronger, more determined. But I still wasn't good enough for my own expectations. I felt I needed more of an edge. So, after I found an article in *FourFourTwo* magazine outlining the "ideal diet for footballers", I followed the diet regimentally. In itself, this wasn't a bad thing. It wasn't particularly restrictive; it involved lot of wholegrain carbs, proteins, vegetables, and dairy, so it was definitely sustainable and healthy. Everything was fine until, in one particular football game, I picked up a minor injury.

I'd fully prepared for the game as I always did. I led the team onto the pitch. I played as though it was a cup final. I had the desire to win embedded deep inside me. I went up to head the ball midway through the game and got pushed from behind. This wasn't unusual, as many girls weren't prepared to head the ball and so they resorted to trying to win the ball through foul play. I ended up on the ground, noticing a slight pain in my back. I didn't let it bother me. I got up, took the free kick, carried on, and ran my socks off for the remainder of the game.

It was only a few days later that I knew something was up. The pain in my upper back on the left-hand side got worse and worse until it became unbearable. I had to go to the doctor because the pain was so bad, and I later found out that I'd torn a ligament. I got no release from it, just ongoing pain. I could feel a constant dull throb, and the pain intensified with every movement I made. I spent days with hot water bottles on my back and the only form of physical activity I could undertake was walking.

I had never experienced an injury before, and I found the process demoralising and difficult. It felt like my teammates were improving around me and I had no way of catching them up.

I mentioned that I was feeling really down, but that was dismissed by a GP I wasn't familiar with at my doctors' surgery. She figured it was because I couldn't play the game I loved. I had no way of releasing my anxieties and emotions on the football pitch and this proved to be detrimental to my mental health.

I had physiotherapy twice a week, which involved passing a gentle electrical current through my muscle. My physio, Sarah, advised me to also do some rehabilitation work in the gym to help aid my recovery. Sarah was, in fact, the mum of one of my old friends from Pixmore. On one particular appointment, I removed my shirt and lay face down on the bed as usual. She then commented on my weight. 'You're awfully thin, Ruth,' she said to me quietly, her hands on my back. 'I can feel your bones.'

I tensed a little. 'I've just been training in the gym a lot,' I replied.

21

I knew I looked and felt frail, but I didn't want to talk about it. It made me feel self-conscious and uncomfortable. I had been restricting my food a huge amount – more than my initial diet regime prescribed – because I hadn't been doing much exercise. I genuinely believed that I didn't deserve to eat. I had completely removed anything deemed "unhealthy" from my diet, and my calorie intake (which I was meticulously counting) had dramatically decreased. I was probably eating 700 calories a day, and as a growing and active teenager, this was dangerously low.

I would scrutinise my parents' cooking and complain if they added too much oil. I was so fixated on this mindset. I wasn't struggling with anorexia, but I did have a very unhealthy obsession with food. I didn't intentionally lose weight – it was just about control. In fact, I didn't realise I had lost weight until people – sports teachers in particular – started to make comments. It's hard when you see yourself every day in the mirror. Changes are too subtle and everything looks "normal". But to people who hadn't seen me for a while, like Sarah, my weight loss was a shock.

When I was allowed to train again, I over-trained. I was in the gym most days. I would run before school at 6.00am and walk as far as I could every day. I started to lift weights and I'd sit on the exercise bike for hours. It gave me a personal focus. I didn't care how I looked or what I weighed – that wasn't why I was doing it. It gave me some kind of control in my life while everything else was going to pot. It gave me an element of comfort.

I did, however, become scarily thin. Now, when I look at photos of me taken during that time, I'm horrified. My bones stuck out everywhere, my face was drained of colour, and I looked so weak and fragile – like I would collapse at any moment. I had a six-pack that most would be proud of, and I liked the definition of my muscles, but I got down to about 40kg in weight and there was not an ounce of fat on my body. I was cold all the time; my hands were blue and my cheeks were pallid and ghost-like. Every piece of clothing swamped my body.

I think eating disorders and restricted eating are really common in sportspeople and athletes. There's a pressure on people to look the part, to be at the ideal weight to perform at their peak, and although this is important, it can be really dangerous too. I'm pretty sure I wouldn't have suffered with any issues with food if I hadn't been sporty. The repercussions of food restriction can be catastrophic, as I unfortunately found out.

My injury did slowly ease off, which meant I could start playing football again and run and train more vigorously in the gym. But despite this, I soon realised that I was really struggling to enjoy anything in my life. Even when I played football I felt weak and flat, and I didn't get the buzz I'd always had and craved on the pitch. I just didn't care about it anymore. My passion and desire to play the beautiful game had dissipated. Instead, all I really wanted to do was curl in a ball and hide away. This was unlike anything I had ever felt before and filled me with fear and confusion.

I didn't want to have to face the world because I was scared of what people would think of me and how I'd changed. Why wasn't I smiling all the time?

It was exhausting being around people, pretending that everything was okay. I was almost surprised that people couldn't see this black cloud hanging over me, because it felt so real and so physical. I hated that I felt victimised by my own feelings. I didn't understand them. Why did I feel so helpless?

I spent hours and hours and days and days on my own. I would walk or run for miles, listening to music to try to escape from my head. I would physically exhaust myself so that as soon as my head touched the pillow, I would fall into a deep sleep. Sleep was my respite, but I would wake up with no energy. I continued to restrict my eating.

One Monday, after a number of confusing and challenging weeks, I refused to go to school. The thought of speaking to anyone – or dealing with anything – was just too daunting. I just cried. Dad, clearly concerned, decided to ring the GP and book an emergency appointment. I could barely speak and was utterly confused by the feelings I was having. Both my parents came to the appointment but we didn't really have any idea what we were doing or what to expect. My dad, ever the practical man, wrote down what I had been feeling and going through:

Flat

Down

Weight loss

Lack of motivation

No enjoyment

Difficulty socialising

He might as well have copied the common symptoms for depression from the NHS website.

I sat in the waiting room, scanning the place. I read the flu posters over and over. There were a lot of old people around. It felt wrong being there. How on Earth was a doctor going to help the way I was feeling?

When my name appeared on the screen above us, I followed my parents to Dr Taylor's room. My dad knocked on the door and we went inside.

My heart was pounding in my chest. This was an experience I'd never had before.

Following introductions, my dad showed the doctor the piece of paper. I refused to speak really. I just nodded and shook my head at the right times. I had very little energy and I was embarrassed about being here. 'You're not a happy bunny, are you?' said Dr Taylor, looking right at me.

I cringed inside. My shoulders dropped, my head dropped, and a single tear dropped down my face, despite my doing everything I could to stop it happening.

I couldn't really believe what he had just said. Of course I wasn't happy! I had an enormous cloud of darkness hanging over me. It felt like he was undermining my issue; it seemed like he thought I ought to be happy. It also seemed like it was easy for him and my dad and my mum and everyone else in the world to act happy – and here I was, struggling to even smile. I felt so alone in this.

I know now – although it was hard to see at the time – that he genuinely cared, although it was hidden somewhat behind his authoritarian manner. The 10-minute appointment time cap was far exceeded which shows he took the time to learn about what was going on with me. He really wanted the best for me.

This appointment was the first time I'd heard the words "clinical depression". I couldn't really believe it was being used to describe me. Why should I have been depressed? I was academic, sporty, popular, and I'd had a good upbringing ... it just didn't make sense. It didn't feel fair.

He immediately prescribed the antidepressant fluoxetine (Prozac), a selective serotonin reuptake inhibitor. This was despite the fact that suicidal thoughts were the most prominent side effect in under-18s. I wasn't made aware of this, but even if I had been I don't think I would've changed anything. I didn't have a choice. I was only young. I didn't really know what depression was. I didn't even know what mental illness was. I didn't know much about suicide. I just didn't understand any of it.

I was referred to CAMHS for therapy, but this meant being put a six-month waiting list. And so I saw no other options other than to follow the doctor's advice, take the medication, and wait and see what happened next.

CHAPTER 3

JUST SMILE

The next few weeks were the most difficult I had ever had to endure.

I couldn't face going back to school. My dad emailed my Head of Year, Mr Turner, explaining the situation. He told him that I was in a really bad place and found it very hard to deal with daily life. By this point I was just crying and crying non-stop in my bedroom. I couldn't enjoy anything.

The response wasn't great. Mr Turner replied and told my dad that I needed to be in school by law. But I just didn't feel up to it. I remember thinking to myself that if I'd had a physical illness like chicken pox or tonsillitis, I'd have been given the necessary time out to recover. But because this was about my mental health, it was somehow different.

I couldn't deal with life at home. I was barely even socialising. How was I meant to cope with being in school, let alone do the work?

Mr Turner arranged a meeting for the following day and invited me, my parents, and the school nurse. It felt like I was fighting a losing battle as I sat at the long boardroom table. Everyone around me was forcing me to be in an environment where I didn't feel comfortable.

To their credit, my parents didn't know any better, so they just assumed that being in school was the right thing for me; it seemed to work for other students in similar situations. In my head I was screaming at them all to not make me go to school, but I had lost my voice. Despite this whole meeting being about my wellbeing, I was only asked one question.

'How do you feel about being in school?' Mr Turner asked.

I stayed quiet for a second, then choked out, 'I just can't deal with the social side of it.' I immediately burst into tears. I was inconsolable.

Everyone just looked at each other, no one quite knowing what to do. After a few awkward moments, Mr Turner told the nurse to take me downstairs while he continued to talk to my parents.

I didn't get on with her. 'Come on, Ruth, just smile,' she said. Anger boiled up inside me – it was like she didn't have any understanding whatsoever of what I was going through.

Despite my anger, however, I kept quiet. Of course I didn't agree with what she said, but I just didn't have the energy to even reply. I'm sure that if I had, I would've got worked up and walked out. Instead I bit my tongue and tried to block out what she was saying.

No matter how much I fought against it, the decision was made that I needed to be in school. And so the next few weeks were absolute hell. I didn't actually go to any lessons; I just had to go into school every day to keep the structure in my life. This was so that when I did start going to lessons, it would be an easier transition for me. At least, that's what I was told.

I would wake up every day with an overwhelming sense of dread and fear. I would cry while eating breakfast, I would cry during the whole 40-minute car journey, and I would cry to the school nurse, who I had to sit with for 30 minutes while Mum waited in the carpark. We'd then drive all the way home, and yet again I'd be in floods of tears. We repeated this cycle every single day.

I felt weaker than I'd ever felt before, both physically and mentally. My face was gaunt and pale all the time. I got no enjoyment out of anything whatsoever, so didn't see the point in doing anything. I didn't meet with friends after school and I didn't enjoy football or hockey. I would often just walk or run for miles on end, just to pass the time. I just waited for the daytime to tick away so I could fall into a deep sleep.

I kept myself very much to myself and refused to let people know I was struggling. I saw it as a sign of weakness and feared everybody's judgement. I think I did a good job of hiding it. I didn't open up to my friends, family, coaches, or teachers; I just carried on as though there was nothing wrong. My school work stayed consistent throughout, so it was hard for anyone to realise that something was up. I have no idea how I was able to focus with so much going on in my head, but it was kind of a release for me to get my head down and work. It brought back a little bit of the "old me", the girl I was before my diagnosis.

This was really comforting. I'd always found school work relatively easy, and although my depression made most other parts of my life virtually impossible, I was still able to learn my Latin keywords and revise for my German speaking exam. I missed lessons due to being with the nurse or being at home, but all the work was sent to me at home and I'd get it done straight away.

I guess I was scared that I would lose the foothold I'd created for myself. I didn't want my depression to cause my grades to drop. I didn't want it to stop me from achieving what I wanted to achieve. Even on really bad days – when even leaving my bed was a challenge – I got it done.

When I spoke to one of my ex-teachers recently about this time in my life, she said she had a feeling something was up, but just assumed I didn't want to talk about it. Another said they had no idea whatsoever. If I'm honest, I would've loved someone to say to me, 'Do you want to have a chat?' but instead there we were, pretending that everything was okay. I battled on alone.

At the end of December 2013 I made the painful decision to quit football. It wasn't an easy decision. At the start of the month I'd been selected to attend a training camp for the England Independent Schools Football Association at St George's Park in Burton upon Trent. I shared the pitch with so many footballing greats. I stayed in the same hotel and ate in the same canteen. And yet despite the fact that this was the pinnacle of my footballing career – and though I tried to take it all in and appreciate the experience – deep inside I knew that this also marked the end of it. I no longer got any form of enjoyment out of the game that had shaped my childhood.

I couldn't join in with the camaraderie within my team. Pretending I was happy all week at school, and then having to do it during the evenings and weekends at football too, was just too much for me. I was so exhausted. I became weak on the ball. I could no longer do bullet shots, hold up the ball, or do heavy tackles, and I had little left without them.

Depression had taken away my appetite, along with my desire. The ground had been pulled from beneath my feet and I was left feeling empty and guilty. I was no longer "the girl who plays football" and so I felt that I lacked all identity and purpose. When people asked me why I quit, I answered with, 'I just wasn't enjoying it anymore.' Most people left it at that. Some replied with, 'But you were so good!' for which I didn't really have an answer. I didn't think I was good anymore. I used to pull players up. I led from the top. But now, I was convinced I was just dragging everyone down. Football became a trigger word for me. It brought to me a world of pain. I couldn't even watch *Match of the Day* anymore.

Eventually I started attending just one lesson a day at school. I'd then go back to see the nurse and then go home.

That was all I could deal with. At the end of lessons I'd become tearful, and because I had to pretend that everything was okay throughout the class, I guessed that my classmates would think it was childish to randomly start crying my eyes out. So I had to hold it in.

I was quiet in class. I didn't answer any questions. I just got my head down, completed the work, and left. I didn't talk to anyone. I felt like a robot.

I was unsure of how much my teachers knew at the time, except for a select few. If I was late to a lesson – say, for example, because I'd initially refused to go and the nurse had had to persuade me otherwise – I would hand a slip of paper to the teacher saying that I'd been with her. I'm certain that some of my teachers could've guessed from my demeanour that I was struggling severely with my mental health, but no one ever said anything to me. For me, my depression was just a huge elephant in the room. But perhaps I hid it better than I thought.

Whenever I wasn't in school and me and my mum went out somewhere, I was just riddled with guilt. I thought people would think I was skiving or just pretending I was ill. My attendance had always been 100%, so it was hard to accept being in and out of school without feeling guilty.

Over the coming weeks I gradually did more and more lessons per day (a full timetable had six lessons per day). Some weeks I took a step back because I just felt unable to deal with the social side of things. I was exhausted. I didn't want to constantly have to wear a mask. I was pretending I was someone I wasn't anymore. I became incredibly self-conscious about what people thought of me. *What did they think of how I looked? Why did they think I wasn't smiling?*

I became a full-time student again over the course of a month or two. In my own time I caught up with all the school work I had missed. A few people asked about my absence, but I didn't let anybody in. I just said I'd been ill. Of course, struggling with depression is being mentally ill, but I didn't think this was a thing at the time. I thought all illness was purely physical, as many still do now. My weight loss lent itself to this theory, so they asked no further.

I was ashamed of what I'd been through. But I imagine if I'd been suffering with a physical illness – that wouldn't have been the case then.

My form tutor, Mr Higgens, made a conscious effort to welcome me into school on my first full day back as I waited outside the medical room. He clearly knew what I had been through, and was incredibly understanding and genuine. I guess this made me feel an element of accomplishment, although it took me a while to acknowledge it.

My parents, Lynn and Andrew, are lovely people. My dad has always had that competitive trait and I've clearly inherited it. He is a dentist and has always been a high achiever. He always puts other people first, and has an incredibly practical approach to life. He loves sorting things out. Whether it's spring cleaning, negotiating insurance policies, or filing bank statements, he enjoys taking control and organising things. My mum, on the other hand, is the complete opposite (it's clear to see just by looking at their respective sides of the bedroom!). They met at Birmingham University and both studied dentistry, but Mum dropped out after three years. She's had various charity job roles since. Mum's pretty laid back and relaxed; she spends her time walking our dog, sewing, and reading. They both put me and Becky first in everything they do. They support us in everything and they're top parents in all that they provide us with.

But what they do sometimes struggle with is expressing their emotions. They both lost their long-term jobs in the space of a year, but they didn't once speak to me over the dinner table about how all this made them feel. Instead, they discussed the next practical steps towards finding new jobs, what they would do with the cars, and how they would pay for the house and bills. I just sat there while they talked about these things, thinking that we were a world away from each other in terms of communication.

I wonder – considering everything that's happened with me – if either of them ever suffered from a mental illness, would they talk more about how they're feeling?

CHAPTER 4

UNSTOPPABLE

Medication is hit and miss for a lot of people, but luckily for me it worked. I didn't have any side effects and it took about a month for the medication to really come into effect.

By April 2014, I was becoming the girl I once was. I had a new-found strength in my own abilities and a confidence that I'd never had before. There was now a huge hole in my life where football used to be, but I tried to fill the void with other activities. I focused my attention on running, cycling, and strength training in the gym. I ranked 200th in England for cross-country and joined a local cycling club. That summer I cycled the width of the country with my dad over the course of three days. Football had always been our shared hobby so naturally our relationship had moved further apart when I quit playing. It felt like it was never the same again.

I really enjoyed improving myself and homing in on the mental strength I had developed in these other activities, but the buzz was never quite the same as when I was on the football pitch.

My CAMHS appointment finally came around – months after I initially needed it back in October. I remember the particular carpark we parked in town was called Lurke Street, and I still feel sick when I park there now because it brings it all back. We had an introductory family appointment. The waiting room was filled with kids' toys and books. As a mature 15-year-old, I thought this was childish and patronising. We had an introductory family appointment in a room upstairs led by a psychologist and a family support worker. I found the meeting awkward and very tick-boxy, going through our family history and relationships.

My parents knew what I'd been through; they'd been by my side and had been supportive of me. But they found it difficult, not knowing the right thing to do or say. It's entirely understandable – I think we all just wanted to forget about it and move on with our lives. We wanted to put these awful experiences well behind us.

They offered me a course of Cognitive Behavioural Therapy (CBT) which revolved around challenging the negative thoughts I'd had, but I decided to decline it. I just believed that someone out there needed it a lot more than I did. I imagined a young girl sitting in her room crying, just as I once had. I imagined what it would be like for her if she was offered this glimmer of hope. I pictured the scene in my head: I saw her parents knocking on her bedroom door. Her mother would peep round and say, 'We've got some good news – your appointment with CAMHS has been moved forward to tomorrow. It was going to be a nine-month wait.'

Plus, in all honesty, I didn't want anything to do with the health services anymore. I wanted to get on with my life. My parents agreed with this decision and respected it. I'd got through this massively challenging bout of depression on my own, with the help of medication. And so being offered professional therapeutic support long after I believed I needed it felt like having salt rubbed into my healing wounds. Depression had been a new experience for me, but it was something that only struck once, right? Why did I need therapy now that I'd recovered? It didn't make sense to me. No one had ever told me otherwise.

I learnt so much about mental illness. I was so young, and I'd not even come across the word "depression" before unless it was used in a "this weather is depressing" kind of way. But I had learnt that depression was an actual illness, that medication could be used to treat it. I learnt about the hormones in my brain and the impact of exercise on mental health. Through my experiences I also developed a level of empathy for anyone who was having a bad day or going through a tough time. Most importantly for me, I realised that depression could strike anyone at any time.

I now cringed inside and felt slightly offended when someone said they were "depressed" when really they meant sad. Comparing the two is like equating a puddle to the sea. The magnitude of depression, an illness, is unparalleled to that of sadness, an emotion.

I felt so well in myself that I stopped taking my fluoxetine a few weeks before the doctor advised me to do so. I hated the taste of the stuff and I hated having to take a medication to make me feel well. It was so unfair that none of my other classmates had to do this! Despite what I'd learnt, relying on medication still made me feel weak.

During my next review appointment, I told Dr Taylor that I had stopped taking my tablets, and he accepted my decision. 'I wouldn't have kept you on the medication much longer, anyway,' he told me with a smile. 'I'm just pleased that you're clearly a world away from the timid girl I first encountered.'

My sister was at university throughout the majority of my struggle. Sometimes I went up to visit her, or she would come home for holidays or during weekends, but it was very hard to connect. I struggled to open up to her about my feelings. She was supportive nevertheless, but I imagine she felt powerless, and perhaps even the slightest bit responsible.

I went on to achieve nine A*s and two As in my GCSEs at the end of Year 11, despite missing several months of lessons during Year 9. We all went out for breakfast on results day, all four of us as a family, and it felt just like old times. I walked past loads of other kids in the street holding that crisp piece of paper that potentially determined our futures, and knew I'd done pretty well in my school – and probably in the country. Mr Turner had peeped over my shoulder as I opened my envelope and said 'With those results, Ruth, you can do anything.' I smiled at him and I believed him. But most importantly for me, I felt I had done Mum and Dad proud. I thought back to that initial family meeting we had on that boardroom table following my diagnosis. It felt a world away.

But at this point my results were unimportant, as my greatest achievement that summer was sharing my mental health story publicly for the first time.

It started when I posted a video on Facebook. It focused on how I had used the gym as a safe space to develop myself both physically and mentally, and how sport was the vehicle I'd used to help me to bounce back from my bout of depression.

The video started with photos of me playing football as a youngster, with the words "football was my passion" appearing across the screen. I wanted to reiterate how important football was to me, so the clip showed images of me as the captain of my club and a representative of England Independent Schools FA. As the music reached its climax, a photo of me in a vest appeared on-screen. In it I looked stick thin. The video then went on to explain the injury I picked up in 2013, my weight loss, and my subsequent depression diagnosis, which lead to me quitting football.

I wanted to make sure that the video focused on the positives. I didn't wallow in how hard everything was; I didn't go on about how tough school was or any of that. Instead, I focused on how I used sport to get back to stability.

'Slowly, I built up my strength, growing stronger every day – both mentally and physically,' I explained in the video.

There was then a clip of me lifting some weights, which was a huge contrast compared to the original photo. It showed just how far I'd come.

At the end of the video I announced that I would be making a return to the game I loved. Behind the scenes I had been looking for women's football teams, and I was excited that I had started taking steps towards playing again. For me, this marked a full and conclusive recovery.

After hockey training one Monday night, I was just packing away my stuff when Miss Gilbert, my hockey coach, came over.

'Hi, Ruth. I saw the video you posted the other night. It brought a tear to my eye,' she said. 'We've had a chat in our faculty meeting and we all think you'll be the worthy winner of the Legacy of 2012 Award.'

The Legacy of 2012 Award was given to a student who inspired others through their involvement in sport (as a continuation of the *Inspire a Generation* campaign from London 2012). I was genuinely shocked by the response – I felt proud for the first time in a long time.

'Aw wow!' I said. 'I just needed to get it out there, I think. I just want people to know what could be going on behind a smile.'

'Well, we'd love you to share the video at the Sports Awards in a few weeks,' Miss Gilbert smiled at me. 'Would you be happy with that?'

'Of course, it would be a pleasure,' I replied, smiling back at her. I'd never been to the Sports Awards before, and I was truly humbled that I'd even been considered for this accolade. I later found out that I'd won the coach's Player of the Season too. I was so happy. I really had turned a corner in my life. I had kicked depression in the arse.

That awards evening remains my proudest. I waited in the audience with a mixture of apprehension and excitement. As I sat there, one memory kept replaying in my mind, over and over again. Back in Year 8 we'd had a very special and inspiring assembly run by one of my teachers, Mr Jenkins. His assembly will always stick with me. He'd never taught me or spoken to me back then, so I didn't know much about him. I did know that he'd taught my dad some 30 years before when he went to the school, though. Mr Jenkins had stood in front of the Year 7, 8, and 9 kids, all of whom were staring at him. He spoke about the most vulnerable times of his life, about his battle with leukaemia and how it had very nearly taken his life. There was a raw emotion in his voice. He paused at times to take a breath, clearly close to tears. I was captivated by this man's pure strength, guts, and courage.

I tried to remember that as I waited to go on stage. I knew that 90 per cent of the people in that room would have no idea what I'd been through. I also knew it would be eye-opening for them, because I was known for always smiling and enjoying life. If I did anything that evening, I wanted to emulate Mr Jenkins. I wanted to garner an emotional connection between my story and the audience, just like Mr Jenkins had.

Miss Gilbert stood at the lectern and read a speech outlining my journey from keen footballer and hockey player to a shy individual struggling with her mental wellbeing. She then told the story of my journey back to full health. It was incredible and surreal to hear my story from someone else's perspective. It was a proud, proud moment.

After her speech she played the video I had made. The song I'd chosen was 'Unstoppable' by Sia. Her lyrics – *I'm unstoppable, I'm a Porsche with no brakes* – rang so true to me in that moment.

Miss Gilbert went on to invite me up to the front to receive my award from England netballer, Pamela Cookey, and my PE teacher, Mr Bignell, who happened to be leaving that year. I had to take a breath before I stood up. The applause from the audience was immense, and I had to remind myself that it was me that they were applauding. All I'd done was battle my demons and beat my depression, but it was heartwarming to receive recognition for that.

When the awards had all been handed out and the audience was heading over to get refreshments in the Sixth Form building, the Headmaster, Mr Hall, approached me. I'd always admired Mr Hall. He's one of those people who didn't have to do anything at all to have authority over people. His height probably helped him, but when he spoke he spoke with care, kindness, and genuine interest. He commended my story and bravery that night, and it meant such a lot to me.

When we went over to the Rutherford Building to get refreshments, several others came over and congratulated me too. 'Well done, Ruth,' Mr Higgens smiled.

Someone pulled my ponytail jokily from behind. I looked over my one shoulder, then the other. There stood beaming at me was Mr Marsh, my other hockey coach.

'Well done you,' he said, putting his arm on my shoulder.

'Thanks, Marshy.'

I was incredibly touched by people's comments. In fact, I still am. Just recently I received a message on Twitter from a mum of a student from my school. Her son had won an award that night. She told me that hearing my story and seeing me receive my award had made her just as proud of me as she was of her own kid. Wow.

I'm so glad you're sharing your story in a published book, she wrote in her message. *I've heard your inspirational story, and now others can too.*

I hung around to say goodbye to Mr Bignell. He is just one of those guys who is an all-round good egg. He had taught me for two years, and I'd always felt like we were on the same wavelength. He'd seen me throughout my journey as an outsider looking in, but at least we stood at the finish line together. He hugged me, both of us with tears in our eyes. He didn't need to say much. We just stood in a warm embrace in a moment that I won't ever forget.

I'd finally done something to make myself proud. I cried all the way home.

That summer I started training with a county-level women's side called Hitchin Belles. I'd played against the manager, Laurence, several times when I'd captained Langford Girls, so he knew my potential and I knew I was in the right place to develop as a footballer. This team would be my stepping stone to playing more competitive and ambitious football. Despite having a long way to go to start playing at the level I knew I was capable of, I was elated to be making a return to doing what I loved the most.

I felt strong and confident. And, like Sia, I felt unstoppable.

CHAPTER 5

THE BEST YEAR OF MY LIFE

Year 12 was undoubtedly The best year of my school career. Overcoming adversity left me with newly gained strength, empathy, a quiet confidence, a profound desire to help others, and the determination and aspiration to "go get it" – to reach for the stars and achieve my very best. I listened to Mr Turner and looked at the whole host of opportunities in further education that were within reach because of my grades. Studying medicine was at the top of that list. Regretfully (and I think Mr Bignell would have agreed), I didn't take PE at A Level, and instead immersed myself in the study of biology and chemistry purely to keep the medicine door open. I also studied Latin and English.

The Sixth Form was a very different approach to school life, and one with which I fell in love: free periods, a Sixth Form café, suits instead of uniform, smaller classes, stronger relationships with staff and free use of the gym ... I soon found my feet. I've always felt older than I am (I think being so close to Becky and her friends probably accounts for that) so I was definitely ready to be challenged further both academically and socially.

I'd never really been massively popular – I had just always had a few really close friends and I got on with most people – but in Year 12, I really started to come out of my shell. My relationships developed in turn, and my friendship group expanded. I remember one breaktime really early on in the first term where I just decided to plonk myself in the middle of a group of new students sitting in the café and start making polite conversation. These students subsequently became really close friends of mine throughout the remainder of my school career and they integrated into our ever-expanding group. I was invited to parties and even had a few of my own. I got to know people outside of the classroom and, whether that be midway through a gym session or completely drunk on a Saturday night, I just enjoyed learning about people and socialising.

In October, we had a Latin trip to Rome, Pompeii and Herculaneum, which I was keen to sign up to. To be quite honest, I didn't really know that many of the people going on it and I didn't even know who I would share a room with, but I wanted to fully immerse myself in the Roman culture (and fancied a holiday).

I was sitting on the coach on the way to the airport at about four o'clock in the morning, just rummaging through my bag to check I had everything, when the room-sharing list was passed around. I'd been slightly apprehensive that I would have to share with people in the year above, and so I was amazed to find that my name was already listed in a room with Alice, Amber and Martha, three girls in my class who I'd not spoken to much before. I was the fourth and final name for their room. I glanced up at the same time as Martha and caught her eye; she gave me a warm and caring smile, one that said 'You're with us'. I smiled back and we all started talking, learning more about each other ... and (probably to everyone else's annoyance) we didn't really stop for the entire trip. We laughed harder than I've ever laughed in my life (mostly at inappropriate Roman statues) and I still remember some of the hilarious times we had. Like the time where I asked a member of the public, 'Dov'è il caffè?' in my most authentic and try-hard Italian accent – only to get the response, 'Over there on the left, love' from a man with a strong, Northern, *English* accent. Or the time where we thought that Versuvius was erupting in the middle of the night, when in fact it was just a tram going past our room ... oh, good times ...

Over those 10 days, the four of us (or "The Vestal Virgins", as we liked to call ourselves) built a friendship stronger than most would over years. We just seemed to click. Interestingly, in our DMC (deep, meaningful conversation) on one of our first nights, three out of the four of us opened up about mental health issues, either ongoing or in the past. I felt at home in their company. We're all still pretty close now and, although we've taken our own separate paths, would love to book a 10-day trip to Rome, Pompeii and Herculaneum together, just the four of us, to reminisce over good times.

My studying took a back seat slightly during Year 12, which was fine because only Latin counted towards my final grade in Year 13 (as the only unreformed A Level I was taking) and I felt confident that I'd do okay in that. I guess it was just a year of sorting out our ideas for the future and turning them into a realistic plan, which, for most of us, took the form of a personal statement. Applying for university is the moment in which you turn from a likeable and personable human being into a candidate number and a set of results. I ended up choosing Sports Science as a course (surprise, surprise) – so I could have done a PE A Level after all! I did enjoy the process somewhat. I loved looking around universities up and down the country with my dad and writing a persuasive piece about why I thought they should choose me. I got offers from all five of the universities I applied for – Newcastle, Exeter, Birmingham, Leeds and Brighton (in order of my preference) – and if I achieved AAA or AAB in my A Levels, I'd be able to accept my preferred offer and be on my way. Exciting times ahead!

The university process wasn't the only new thing for me in Year 12; I also had my first interview – in fact, I had two in the space of a week. They were for my school's Senior Monitors – a bit like prefects, I suppose. They helped out at external events, seated students during assemblies and, most impressively, got to wear matching red-embroidered blazers. I'd always looked up to them throughout my school career. The team of 16 individuals worked seamlessly together and always tended to be academic, sporty, good at drama, musical, popular, nice – the whole package. I knew I wanted to apply. The application process involved filling in a form with key examples of where you'd represented the school, what you thought needed improving, what you'd done to make yourself proud ... the usual stuff. I was pleasantly surprised to be given an interview – but also really scared. I had no idea what to expect.

It was a Thursday at 10 o'clock. I sat outside the Headmaster's office in a small waiting area, skimming through visitor brochures that showcased the school. A wave of panic washed over me as I gulped some water – *perhaps I was out of my depth here, perhaps I should just forget about* ... but it was too late. The door to the office opened and Mr Hall gestured for me to make my way inside. I took a deep breath, swallowed, and walked in.

Mr Hall was accompanied by the deputy head pastoral, and Mr White, the Head of Sixth Form. They all shook my hand, and I took a seat opposite them. The room was large and airy, with a wide window that overlooked the playing fields. A single beam of sunlight danced past the blinds. The boardroom table at which we sat was long and intimidating, and I felt very small. I suddenly felt very warm and very scared. I could feel my cheeks going a colour similar to that of the embroidery of the blazer I was hoping to wear one day. Was it really worth it? I wasn't entirely sure if it was actually the right thing for me!

Each member of staff asked a question regarding the role, my application and my ideas. I answered as best I could. I remember almost breaking down on two occasions, not though fear or embarrassment, but once through overwhelming passion for the school (slightly sad I know), and the other because I was asked about my voluntary work at a local counselling service and I vaguely mentioned the struggles

I'd had, which provoked overwhelming emotion that I just about restrained.

None of this mattered though, as I later found out I'd been successful! Mum and I went to John Lewis that same day in order to buy a blazer to be specially decorated with the red trim. Following the second interview five days later, I was also made a House Deputy. It was proving to be a successful – and, most importantly for me, an enjoyable year.

In terms of studying, I didn't find A Levels particularly easy – I don't think many people do! Loads of people that I've spoken to now say they found them harder than university exams. I found biology the most interesting, and my passion for the subject was catalysed (biology pun) by my teachers, Mr Donoghue and Mr Jenkins (who finally taught me 37 years after teaching my dad back in 1980). Mr Donoghue had joined the year before, so he was still relatively new to the school. He had a friendly smile and a very relaxed demeanour. He had a mellow Irish accent (although it was fairly strong when he first taught us – and especially so when he came back from holidays in Dublin). We got on instantly and he offered any support that was needed.

Mr Donoghue was someone always we'd greet in the corridor, and he'd always ask how our weekend was. He was just an all-round good guy; you just knew that from the off. A quick replier to emails, he always did everything to ensure that we understood everything he taught us. In a quiet class, I was often the only person to put my hand up, initiating more participation from my classmates and encouraging others to be more vocal in his lessons. Practicals such as dissecting a heart were always a barrel of laughs, and we'd have occasional "tea and cake lessons" (another Sixth Form perk – my sister's chemistry teacher used to do weekly lessons where members of the class baked cakes to be marked on taste, chemistry-based design, crumb, and texture, but we never went that far!) at the end of term where we could forget about the pressure of the course and get to know each other as people rather than just students.

On results day in Year 12, I opened an envelope that contained a slightly disappointing piece of paper. It read:

Latin: A

English: B

Biology: C

Chemistry: E.

As I've mentioned, however, Latin was the only one that actually counted towards my A Level and I dropped chemistry, so it wasn't disastrous. My teachers were confident that I'd be more than capable of achieving my goal of AAA and begin the next stage of my life, and I, of course, was confident of that too.

CHAPTER 6

RELAPSE

That word. Relapse.

It's a word I genuinely thought wouldn't ever apply to me. I thought I'd never have to experience depression ever again. It was just horrific. Surely I had learnt what I needed to learn from this illness? Surely I could get on with my life, free from the curse of the black dog?

How bitterly wrong I was.

I still remember the day I realised it was all happening again. I remember it as though it was yesterday.

A couple of weeks earlier my gran – or Granny Wendy, as we call her – had gone into hospital, having fallen in the night and broken her hip.

I remember texting her the morning after with no idea of what had happened:

Morning GW, going carol singing tonight at the old people's home. Coffee this week? Love R x

She replied,

Had a nasty fall in the night, Ruth, in hospital now. Enjoy carol singing. Thinking of you. GW

The fact that, even in that situation, she still put me first is testament to her character. I didn't go carol singing that night; I went to visit her in hospital instead.

I felt futile and helpless, seeing her bed-bound and lacking all independence. She is such a strong and determined character, and we've always had a really close bond, so it was hard to see her in pain. I felt that same sense of loss that I'd experienced when Becky left home for university.

I had no idea that this would trigger anything. I remember having a biology end-of-unit test around the same time Granny Wendy went into hospital. I really struggled to revise for it because I spent most of my free periods catching the hospital bus to visit her. The day after this test I spoke to Mr Donoghue and told him my situation. I'd been achieving high marks in my tests so far, but on this one I'd got a D. I think this was the first indication for both me and Mr Donoghue that something perhaps wasn't quite right.

One Thursday in early December 2016, I woke up exhausted, which wasn't unusual. I felt stressed, but in my final year of school – when I had three A Levels to contend with – that didn't surprise me either. But something else felt strange.

As I looked in the mirror I searched for something, anything physical that made me different from yesterday. At first there was nothing, but then I saw it. It was my eyes.

My deep, glassy blue eyes had coal-black circles underneath them, a result of sleepless nights. There was also a single tear in one of them. I was suddenly very fragile again, an emotional pain stabbing me in the heart. I was worthless, useless, and entirely on my own for the second time in my life.

Headphones in and staring blankly out of the bus on my morning commute, I became lost in my thoughts. 'The Climb' by Miley Cyrus came on and I have never felt more connected with a song in any moment. The lyrics, *There's always gonna be another mountain, sometimes I'm gonna have to lose,* felt like they had been written for me. I felt the urge to cry and had to work hard to hold it in.

I was back to the place I feared the most in the world, although some part of me refused to acknowledge it.

All throughout that day at school I was distant, quiet, and flat. My friends might have noticed that something was up, but no one said anything. I needed to talk to someone. I couldn't keep going like this. I was being destroyed from the inside out.

The way I picture mental illness is like an infection that hits the brain. Gradually, once it's messed about with your head, it moves to your limbs, weakening every nerve and vessel in its path, until eventually it reaches your heart, where it destroys every emotion, hope, dream, and aspiration. That's when you need help.

I kept saying to friends that I needed to talk to someone, but didn't have the courage until the afternoon. I decided to approach my biology teacher, Mr Donoghue, who I trusted and got on well with. I had an English lesson which I decided to sacrifice as I thought this was more important. He was supervising his class who were researching independently in the computer suite in the Rutherford Building. I composed myself for 45 minutes, the whole lesson, before approaching him.

I walked up to him when his students had filed out. 'Can I have a chat?' I asked him nervously.

'Of course, no problem,' he said, his Irish twang making me feel slightly more at ease. He patiently waited for me to speak.

We both stood silently for a few moments, until I could bring myself to talk. 'I'm just really struggling,' I managed to force out.

There were tears in my eyes and my voice wavered, but I refused to cry in front of him. I didn't want to look weak.

The irony is, I must've cried to him dozens of times throughout the next few months. But, in this moment, I was vulnerable. I didn't know how much I wanted to disclose to him.

He was standing just a few metres away from me. He was relaxed and appeared at ease with the situation. 'Well, that's okay. We all have a lot of time for you here. You work hard, and I can let your other teachers know to take some pressure off for you. If there's anything at home, or anything else troubling you, I'm more than happy for you to talk to me about it.'

I nodded, but I had to get it across to him that this was about something more than academic stress. I really wished I was just struggling with school; I wished this was something I could cope with. 'I just don't know how many more times I can get hit.' I was babbling now, but I felt I had to.

Again, Mr Donoghue reassured me that he was there if I needed him, but he was in no way forcing me to talk to him. He was careful with what he said, recognising that I was in a bad state. I think he knew that talking about it now or asking me questions would make me cry.

I knew I could trust Mr Donoghue, but I didn't want to say the word "depression" out loud because it meant I had to come to terms with the reality that was slapping me in the face. I knew he wouldn't be judgemental or anything, but I was still scared of how he'd react to me saying, 'I think my depression is back.' I felt kind of ashamed that I had let this happen again. How had I let it creep up on me from behind? It all felt like a sick joke.

Despite taking several steps forward in my recovery and my personal development, I had fallen backwards. People knew my story and they knew how far I'd come. Now the person everyone regarded as strong and inspirational was weaker than ever. I'd failed my friends, my peers, my family, and myself. I couldn't bear to put my parents through it all over again.

When I left Mr Donoghue's room I caught sight of two of my friends, Alice and Amber, in the corridor. I ran to hug them both and broke down into a fit of tears, anger, and fear. They held me tight, asking me what was up, but I was too exhausted to reply. I was ashamed to tell them the truth.

I was in disbelief more than anything. I went to bed that night feeling like I'd been diagnosed with cancer. I know that's a terrible thing to think, but that's exactly how it felt for me.

The following day at school, as I sat with my friends at break time, I felt even worse than the day before. I sat there emotionless, with a dull numbness in my head. I felt like an empty shell. I wasn't listening to what anyone was saying; the volume in the room was overwhelming. I wanted to leave but I didn't move; I stayed where I was, taking sips from my cup of tea, and waiting for break to come to an end.

The social side of school was seriously testing me. Seeing everyone else getting on with their lives made me very uncomfortable. It was as if I was living in a bell jar, as Sylvia Plath so beautifully puts it. A single tear fell down my cheek, followed by another, then another. I held my head in my hands and tried to hide myself from the world. My best friend, Rebekah, consoled me.

'I just cannot deal with this,' I muttered. She didn't say anything; she just gave me a hug. Then she spotted Mr Donoghue on duty in the corner of the room. She knew I'd spoken to him the day before.

When Mr Donoghue came over, I refused to look at him or anyone else. I covered my face with my hands. He crouched down to my level and asked me what was wrong. I repeated what I had just said. 'I just cannot deal with this.'

'Shall we go and have a chat?' Mr Donoghue replied. He stood up and, although it felt like my legs were weighed down with lead, I followed him out of the room. I was aware of dozens of pairs of eyes looking at me.

We went to a small room in the Rutherford Building and I told him everything that was on my mind. I told him how scared I was. I told him I was worried about how much of my life depression would take from me this time. How long would it take to get through this? What would other people think?

Mr Donoghue knew I'd struggled with depression in the past as he'd seen my video at the Sports Awards. I'd always been really chirpy, confident, and bubbly in his lessons when he had taught me in Year 12, so I imagine it was hard for him to see me like this.

We spoke for about 20 minutes and he did what he did best: he listened. His solution was very practical: he immediately helped me reduce my timetable so that I had fewer classes to deal with and therefore less stress. He emailed the Head of Sixth Form, Mr White, to let him know that I was going through a rough time and so he was taking some of the load off me, and reassured me that he was at the end of an email should I need a chat at any time.

It was also in that conversation with Mr Donoghue that he suggested talking to the school nurse (yes, the "just smile" one), who now had a more pastoral role. I did give this a go following our chat, thinking perhaps she had changed or would treat me differently because I was in Year 13, but that wasn't the case. Although I was a more mature and entirely different person to the timid 14-year-old she had first encountered, she spoke to me in the same patronising manner. I decided at this point that it was in my best interest not to speak to her, which Mr Donoghue and the other teachers in my support network respected.

I went back downstairs to the empty canteen. My cup of tea was still on the table. It was now cold.

Over the next few weeks I took up Mr Donoghue's offer and met with him regularly to unload all my thoughts, whether that be during breaktime, lunchtime or before school. We would walk to the staffroom and I'd wait outside while he made us both a cup of tea. He knew I liked a strong brew. This small, simple act made me feel cared for. It meant a lot to me that he had time for me and that we were on the same level. He wasn't a teacher looking down on a student. He was one human being looking out for another. Although he had limited experience of dealing with a student with mental illness, he did all the right things.

Mr Donoghue was incredibly understanding, empathetic, and attentive, and I will always be grateful for the time he devoted to listening to me. If he was ever on break time duty, I would go and sit with him so that I didn't have to deal with my peers.

It was hard to sit there and be unhappy. It was difficult, debilitating, and heartbreaking to watch my friends having banter. Just a couple of months ago I'd have been at the forefront of it all. Depression's crippling grasp had turned me into a person I hated. It changed me, moved me away from the person I had worked so hard to become.

It helped me to have someone to go to if the school day got too much. For this reason, Mr Donoghue became a pivotal person in my journey.

I distanced myself from friends and lacked all concentration in lessons. My attendance dropped massively. I was completely cut off from the world, watching others enjoy their lives in the way I should've been. I was reticent to talk to my parents or my sister. I really didn't want to put them through any more than I already had done. I hid it from them for as long as I could, but eventually Mr White called us all into a meeting at parent's evening. Here I finally opened up to them. School life was becoming too difficult.

'You've seen Ruth's video from the Sports Awards?' my dad asked Mr White midway through the conversation.

'I have, I was there that night. Inspiring,' Mr White replied.

'You can use sport to get you out of this again, Ruth,' Dad said desperately, turning to me. 'It worked last time.'

I stayed silent. I just wished he could take a look inside my head. I wished he could experience a day with my pain. My depression twisted and distorted his words, and my mind translated them: 'Come on, Ruth, go for a run. That'll cure it.'

Obviously, I know now that this wasn't what he meant at all. He was clinging onto what he knew and just wanted the best for me as he always did. But in the moment it felt like a blow to the heart. It just wasn't that simple.

My parents struggle to address emotion, and that made life very hard for me. They have a very practical approach to life, so they were completely out of their comfort zone. Trying to understand what I was going through must have been devastatingly hard for them, and it definitely wasn't their fault. I would never blame my parents for anything – they've sacrificed so much for me and Becky, and I am indebted to them – but it didn't help that I didn't have that understanding at home. In fact, it was potentially detrimental.

With the Christmas break looming, we all hoped that I would soon get some much-needed rest and time out. Hopefully things would look up going into the spring term, and I would go back to the usual bright, enthusiastic, and happy Ruth that everyone knew.

I wished for that more than anyone else in the world. I grasped onto this thread of hope with all I had.

I had waited four months to spend quality time with Becky over her break from university, but I couldn't even sit down and have a chat with her. I always left as soon as we'd eaten dinner to avoid engaging in anymore conversation then was needed. I thought she'd be the first person I'd go to with any problem, considering how close we were (I think a lot of people around me probably thought that too), but since she'd gone to uni we'd been drawn further and further apart without either of us realising it.

To be honest, I felt like everything I said to her had to be positive. I had to tell her I was doing fine, that I had the perfect life, and nothing was ever wrong. I don't know why I did this, but there was something reassuring about it. Maybe I did it to put her mind at ease so that she wouldn't spend time worrying about me. I felt she had enough to worry about at uni. I wanted her to be having the time of her life, and wished her all the happiness in the world.

I isolated myself a lot. I went out alone to run or kick a ball about, and other than that I would stay in my room. And so it took me three weeks to tell Becky exactly how horrendous I was feeling. On that day I'd been crying on my own for about an hour and had reached a breaking point. I felt I couldn't live like this anymore.

I knocked on her door.

'Come in.' She sounded preoccupied, so I was apprehensive about disturbing her.

'Hey, Bec,' I said as I peeped round the door frame. I loved her room. There was always the overpowering scent of clean washing and her favourite perfume. It was never tidy, but never a mess either. It looked homely, like someone relaxed and comfortable lived there. My room, on the other hand, was either a complete and utter bomb site – where catching a glimpse of the carpet was a challenge – or so obsessively tidy it looked like a showroom. It was strange how my mind worked.

'Hey, Ruthie, how you doing?' she asked me.

I looked up from the floor and stared her in the eyes. 'This is just so hard,' I answered. I started to cry again.

This was hopeless. I didn't know what Becky could do. Of course she was supportive, and she wanted the best for her little sister, but I think she found it hard to see me hurting so much. I'm sure she felt powerless, not knowing what she could do to help. She was studying psychology at university, so she had an understanding of depression and a knowledge of the different medication and therapy options there were out there. And so, after a long hug, she searched for some stuff on Google.

She looked up some self-help material and printed some CBT documents, but I didn't really think anything would help me, especially if I had to do it on my own. If all that was required was to think more positively, then surely I'd be doing that already?

Despite this, I was grateful that she was trying to help. Along with Mr Donoghue, it felt like I had someone else on my team fighting alongside me. Although depression made me try to think otherwise, I was never truly alone.

Things were tough on an emotional level, because we were family and it was Christmas time. During the season when so many people are spending time with their family, giving to others and appreciating life, I felt so isolated, like someone was punishing me for something I hadn't done. It was exhausting to keep smiling.

Christmas day at Granny Wendy's house should have been a celebration of her incredible recovery following her hip operation. And yet, I found myself spending most of the day upstairs on my own. I became tired really quickly when I was surrounded by people, even when they were the people I loved most in the world. I went to the kitchen all the time to make everyone tea and coffee all throughout the day, just to get away and spend time on my own and to feel like I was being remotely useful. It frustrated me that we were all receiving pointless presents, ones that we would likely only use once and then throw into a drawer for the next 12 months. I just didn't see the point, not just in Christmas, but in everything. There is a huge expectation to be grateful and happy during this time of year, but I really couldn't exhibit either of those feelings.

The only time my mood lifted just slightly was when Mr Donoghue emailed me on Christmas evening to check how I was getting on. It truly meant the world to know he was thinking about me, despite the fact that he was probably still celebrating with his own family.

Although I really wanted to start 2017 with new hope and a new perspective, January brought with it instead a new depth of darkness that completely enveloped my life and the lives of those around me.

CHAPTER 7

ONE OF THOSE BATTLES

At 17 years old, it was my responsibility to talk to my GP. It was daunting. I had a new doctor following the retirement of my previous one and, after an initial appointment, she referred me back to CAMHS. She also gave me the option of starting medication should things get worse.

Within two days I had called her to give her the go-ahead to prescribe. I was falling deeper and deeper into the darkness and I was out of control.

My eating problems had also taken a turn. Having restricted my food for so long when I was unwell, my body was in desperate need of carbohydrates and fats. And since I'd got back up to a healthy weight by eating a lot, I now mentally had the go-ahead that stuffing your face with food that isn't actually particularly good for you was okay. So I used this as a coping mechanism at times. If I'd had a bad day, I'd eat a packet of Oreos, and that would at least give me some comfort.

'A packet of Oreos? That's not much! I have one every night!' I hear you shout. Well, yeah you're right, that's pretty normal, but that wasn't the end of it. I would have packets of anything and everything. If it comforted me I'd have it. I would then feel overwhelmed with guilt afterwards, but during the binge I was at ease, and that's all I needed at the time.

I guess my weight was slightly controlled because I was an athlete and burnt a lot of it off. But I did start to use other methods so I didn't have to live with the guilt of overindulging. I began to make myself sick several times, and although I was really bad at it, the feeling afterwards was one of relief. I always felt that I'd undone the damage caused (which, of course, I hadn't). I also overdosed on laxatives one day, which was a horrific experience. I refused to go to A&E, though.

Medication should have been my saviour from depression. It had worked in the past, and I was optimistic that it would help me get to where I wanted to be. I thought that was a reasonable assumption. I was put on fluoxetine again and was prescribed 20 mg a day. Having been on 10 mg a day in 2013, starting on 20 mg seemed strange and unnecessary. I wasn't in a good mindset to argue, however, and quite frankly I would've consumed anything to stop my anguish.

But five days later I was in A&E.

On the Friday evening I had just had a shower and was about to leave the bathroom to go into my room when I noticed a razor blade on the side. I had been experiencing such numbness for so many weeks that I just needed to feel something. I reached for the razor, feeling like I was breaking some kind of rule in doing so. But I just didn't care about anything anymore. What did it matter?

I put the razor up against my wrist and moved the blade quickly from one edge to the other. A thin trail of blood followed the direction of my razor. I repeated the action several times, and my arm stung like hell. I clenched my fist and squeezed my eyes shut to try to eradicate the pain. When I had finished, I washed my wrist under the tap. The cool water washed the cuts, and it was somewhat macabre seeing my own blood, diluted, spiral down the plug.

I had never self-harmed before. It had never even crossed my mind before this, but it felt like the right thing to do at that moment in time. The cuts weren't very deep, but there were quite a few of them. Hurting myself didn't relieve my hopelessness, nor did it feel like a release as I had expected. But it didn't make anything worse, which I saw as a positive.

I was certain I was going to tell my parents when I was ready and had plucked up the courage to approach them. But on the Saturday night, while I was sitting in the armchair watching TV in my dressing gown, my dad noticed the cuts on my wrists. He was horrified.

'What's that on your arm, Ruth?' he choked out, dropping to his knees to look closer at my wounds. It was surreal for me to see him on his knees in front of me, but I imagine it was harder for him to see his daughter's wrist covered in cuts. This was the first time I had seen my dad so shaken, so concerned, and so powerless.

'Have you been hurting yourself? Why?' he asked, his face etched with worry.

It pained me to see my dad so disappointed in me – I have always wanted to make him proud. But for the first time I think he really understood how much I had been hurting. And now I'd begun to take it out on myself.

My dad is a naturally practical man, but in this instance all I needed was something emotional; a hug, some reassurance that what I had done was not wrong. I needed to be told that I'd be okay, and I wanted some comfort, a cup of tea maybe. Any form of emotional contact that made me feel loved and cared for – despite the difficulties I was experiencing – would probably have helped.

He took action and rang NHS 111 for some advice, and they then asked to talk to me for an over-the-phone assessment. One of the questions they asked me was about suicidal thoughts. I paused before I answered, because I was ashamed of the thoughts I'd been having a few days before. At one point, when

I'd been alone in my room, I'd envisaged jumping in front of a train. I thought this was the best option for me. I'd conjured up an image of the train track and the train travelling at a hundred miles an hour, hurtling towards me. My thoughts turned even darker: I could visualise mangled metal, bones, and flesh and blood … and then darkness. It was an image clear as glass.

This particularly confused me because, ever since I could remember, I had always tried to make the most out of every single day. I'd always wanted to try new things and to help others, because I believe we only have one life, so we ought to make the most of it. Yet here I was, done with life at 17-years-old. I saw myself with no future, only darkness.

I confirmed to the person on the phone that I'd been having suicidal thoughts, so they advised me to travel to the local hospital and be seen by a psychiatrist within the hour. I was slightly taken aback. I had never had to go to hospital before, and never in a million years did I think I'd end up at A&E for my mental health. I didn't even know you *could* go to A&E for this reason, if I'm honest.

We waited for six hours that night. Eventually I was seen by the psychiatrist on duty at about 2.00am. During the first few hours I cried on and off, just sitting there watching patients come in and out. Things felt very serious – and I was scared. I was scared of what I'd done and scared of what would happen next. My dad sat silently next to me. He had to ask the receptionist several times, to make sure they'd not forgotten about me.

The hospital was incredibly warm, and at one point I went outside to get some fresh air. There was a man smoking a cigarette, who I acknowledged with a nod. I could smell the stench of alcohol on his breath. He asked me why I was at A&E, because I looked "perfectly fine to him". I was scared about how he would react to my telling him I was there for my mental health, and so I should've been.

He laughed at me. 'You're in A&E to see a psychologist?' he said, sounding shocked.

I went back inside. I felt stupid and wanted to go home.

My mum was in Yorkshire for the weekend staying with my grandma, but my dad called her and let her know the situation. She decided to drive back immediately, so I spoke to her on the phone while she stopped at a service station.

'I may have hit rock bottom, but I guess at least it can only go up from here,' I tried to cling onto some hope as I spoke to her. In that moment I imagined my life to be a positive quadratic graph. In it I was sitting right at the vertex, about to embark on the steady climb ahead.

I felt bad for my mum having to drive 170 miles just to be with me. I didn't feel like I needed her, or my dad, or anyone. Through no fault of their own, they couldn't give me the emotional support that I needed, so I felt better off alone. I just wanted to curl up into a ball in the darkness. I certainly didn't want to be in a hospital.

We were transferred to the psychiatric waiting area after about four hours (my mum had driven all the way back by this time) and I was the last to be seen. The waiting area was, in fact, just an out-of-use ward. The walls were white and there were nurses scampering around looking stressed. I had my blood pressure taken, although I feel like this was just to pass some time. There were four other patients waiting alongside me. It was hard to tell what was wrong with them just by looking at them, and I am certain they probably thought the same about me. They were higher on the priority list and thus seen before me, which meant that they were in a worse place than I was.

This thought sickens me even today. I had self-harmed and was having suicidal thoughts, and yet these people still needed more help than I did. I really do hope they are doing okay now. I'll never know.

One of the nurses was clearly concerned about the infinitely long length of time we'd been waiting, so she offered us a cup of tea. The tea was tepid, grey in colour, and presented in stained teacups. It was disgusting, and I only took a few small sips. In any other situation, such a small gesture could've changed my mindset just a tiny bit. It could've made me feel slightly more relaxed and cared for. Instead I just felt sick. I was tempted to call Mr Donoghue and ask him to make me a decent, strong cup of Yorkshire tea.

After a horrifically long six-hour wait, my name was finally called out. I was led to a room where my parents were told to wait outside, as I was required to chat to the psychiatrist alone. The room was white, plain, and clinical. There were two soft chairs opposite each other and a coffee table equipped with a box of tissues. There was an eerie silence, a heavy contrast from the frantic and buzzing waiting room. I was, however, cruelly reminded that I was in hospital by the acrid smell of disinfectant.

The psychiatrist introduced herself as Elaine, who proceeded to talk me through the Mental Health Assessment. She was a large woman with a kind face, but she looked stressed and very tired. She was wearing casual clothes – a pair of jeans and a loose shirt. The NHS lanyard around her neck was the only thing that set us apart. I did feel like just another patient on a conveyor belt, bringing her one step closer to the end of her shift.

The assessment lasted 45 minutes, and it was ultimately a questionnaire about my past. She asked me about my childhood, family situation, any traumas, friendship circles, any substance abuse, self-harm, and suicidal thoughts. She was, she told me, trying to get an idea of the situation I had found myself in. She didn't look up from her writing much. She wasn't listening; she was just hearing. She was just another doctor – it was really nothing more than that.

Quite quickly she realised that self-harming – or indeed thinking I was better off dead – was quite unusual for me. It didn't take a genius to work that out. We didn't really discuss what had caused me to feel this way. Instead, we just talked about how to keep myself safe from here onwards. She recommended techniques such as flicking an elastic band on my wrist or holding an ice cube to emulate the pain of cutting. She invited my parents in at the end, and the last question she asked was if I felt safe to go back home that night without harming myself.

I wish I could've said yes confidently. But I couldn't promise I was 100 per cent safe, as I knew I still had access to the razors. That's why she gave me the option of staying overnight in hospital. Although there were no beds in the adolescent Mental Health Unit, I could've stayed in the children's ward, where I would have to be watched the whole time.

I said I would go home, mostly for my parents' sake. I couldn't bear to put them through any more pain.

I was told that I would be called by the CAMHS crisis team later that morning, who would then see me for an assessment later in the week. The psychiatrist hugged me when we left, which although felt slightly off, gave me some comfort. It made me feel that she genuinely believed in me, certainly more than I believed in myself.

There was silence in the car on the way home. I felt awful for having put my parents through such an ordeal. Once they'd gone to bed, I sat in the sitting room with the TV on as silent noise. It dawned on me that this was getting serious, that I really did need help. I was becoming a danger to myself, and no doubt to others too. I really hated being the centre of attention when I was struggling.

We'd got home at about 4.00am and I was truly exhausted. I had a disjointed sleep and woke up at 8.00am with the same black cloud hanging over me. Although sleep is a wonderful time to escape, it is also a portal to tomorrow which just filled me with infinite dread and fear.

As I sat on the sofa that morning with my dad, nothing felt easier. If anything, it felt harder, because now there was an awkward atmosphere. Neither of us wanted to talk about the night before.

At 11.00am my dad asked, 'Are you playing football today?'

'I don't know,' I replied. Every single part of me said "no". My body ached, my head hurt, I hadn't eaten, and I was mentally drained. But a small voice told me to do it – to push past the barriers that were stopping me.

And so I went.

I had never dreaded a football match in my life, so this was strange for me. I felt unworthy and weak in the car on the way there. My dad agreed to talk to my manager, Laurence, and let him know what had happened the night before. We agreed that it was just like letting a coach know about a niggling injury or strain, although 100 times harder. I stayed quiet while we warmed up and I just focused on the game. I couldn't hide the fact that I felt awful, but I could at least have a ball at my feet and lift some of the weight off my shoulders.

When I went to collect a ball that had been overhit, I had a chat with Laurence, who was putting the corner flags in.

'It's just one of those battles we sometimes have to fight, Ruth,' he said, putting his arm around me. 'I'm proud of you for making an effort today, when it's clearly a real struggle for you.'

Playing football that day was harder than most will appreciate. When depression is at its most powerful, it demotivates you. When getting out of bed it's like your duvet is weighed down with a thousand tons. Talking to people is a nightmare. Nevertheless, I got it done that day. Every shout from the sideline had been a positive one. I didn't play my best – far from it – but I was at least able to let out my frustration and anger. During half time – and whenever the ball went off the pitch and I stopped playing – my focused mindset switched off just for a moment. That's when the darkness overpowered everything again.

But I wasn't going to let this illness destroy my passion for the second time. For more or less 90 minutes, I could be myself once again, and forget about everything beyond the confines of those white lines.

I was actually grateful I went to A&E that night because it sped up the process of getting the help that I needed. I was seen by the CAMHS team two days later instead of several months later (which would have been my original referral from my GP).

The appointments were useful up to a point, but I wasn't given much advice. We talked about keeping myself safe, who to call, and where to go if I felt the same way again. It didn't help me uncover the underlying issues as to why I felt like this.

I also saw an eating disorder team through CAMHS, although I was never given any real diagnosis. I stopped going because I couldn't afford to keep getting the train to Luton, and it really didn't feel like anything at all was helping. They were trying to treat me for an undiagnosed eating disorder, but my underlying issues – i.e. the reasons why I was depressed and therefore why I was using food as a coping mechanism – weren't explored. I didn't want to continue to feel patronised and have another label attached to my already complicated case.

My last appointment with the crisis team was on the following Thursday. It was a bright, sunny morning, and I was in an unusually good mood. Obviously that's what they saw, and so they released me to see the normal (non-crisis) CAMHS team instead. This meant fewer, less-intense appointments. Looking back, I think this was a mistake. One good day doesn't mean you're okay, and equally a smile doesn't mean you're not crying on the inside. An alcoholic can be sober one day – does that mean they're cured?

I do, however, appreciate that hundreds of other young people were in a worse place than me and needed that acute help a lot more than I did. I suppose the 0.7 per cent of the NHS total budget that goes towards CAMHS (at the time of writing, according to the charity Young Minds) can't really stretch far enough.

I had yet another assessment with a psychiatrist from the CAMHS team. I struggled to understand her strong Polish accent, and I knew exactly where she was going with a lot of what she was saying. She prescribed me sertraline, another selective serotonin reuptake inhibitor. She started me on 50mg a day (although I later found out I should've started on 25mg a day). She told me she'd increase this drug by 25mg every two weeks, to reach the peak at two weeks. I hesitantly agreed, and started the course that same day.

Sertraline was another mistake. Having taken the drug for three days, I started dissociating and having suicidal thoughts. They are so hard to describe to someone who's never experienced them. Whether they're fleeting or permanent, they're so difficult to deal with. They were powerful and impossible to ignore. It's not wanting to live, but not wanting to die either. I guess like some kind of suicide limbo.

I vividly recall the first time I almost gave in to them. Three nights after starting sertraline, I crept downstairs, entirely numb of emotion. My bare feet pressed on the ice-cold kitchen tiles, and my devil-possessed hands delved into the medicine drawer. It was as though they were completely detached from my body, and yet my poorly mind was ordering them to do it. I took all 40 sertraline tablets into the dimly lit living room and slumped into a chair. The TV was on but I couldn't hear a thing. My hands trembled and tears filled my eyes.

Do it.

Don't.

Those words ping-ponged around my head for well over an hour, but time had no meaning. When you're that close to contemplating ending your own life, the clocks stand still. I tried to text a few friends saying I was in a bad place, but everybody was busy. My dad was at the pub with his friends and my mum was asleep upstairs. I didn't want to wake her. I was alone.

I had so much potential, so many aspirations, and so much support. But I was plagued by an illness that no one could see.

Something made me make a definitive decision that night. Whatever it was – maybe it was my family, maybe my friends; maybe it was some glimmer of hope. I'm not quite sure, but whatever it was, I am immensely grateful for it. I got myself through this crisis and breathed a sigh of relief that I had resisted the urge.

I couldn't trust myself. I was scared. I cried myself to sleep that night just like most nights, my pillow was soaked with tears. I lay on my front so my parents couldn't hear my pain.

The following day at school was tough. I could barely leave my house that morning, but somehow, I dragged myself out. I took the packet of tablets with me, as I still had strong suicidal urges, and then messaged a friend later that night, telling her that I had brought them in. She did entirely the right thing – she went to the deputy head the following day and told him what had happened. I can't imagine how much of a burden it must have been, trying to keep this information to herself.

At my CAMHS appointment the following day, they told me they'd liaised with the deputy head. For my own safety, I had to take several weeks out of school. I called the psychiatrist the same afternoon and told her I wasn't taking sertraline ever again.

I was truly mortified. Depression was beginning to take hold of me physically as well as emotionally. I was wasting away, no longer able to thrive in the school environment I loved. I was angry at myself for feeling this way, angry for telling my friend I had brought in the medication. I was angry at the world.

Day after day, I isolated myself. My mum took time off work to be with me; we walked the dog, went for coffee, and tried to stay positive. It was incredibly difficult. My parents had no idea how to deal with my illness. They asked questions all the time; perhaps they felt that they ought to. But even if I was having a bad day I wouldn't tell them. It was too complex; my problems were beyond their understanding. It's not because they were unintelligent or didn't care about me, far from it, but because they just couldn't empathise.

I continued to email Mr Donoghue when I was out of school keeping him updated on what was going on with me and how I was feeling daily. He gave me a tiny fragment of light every day. No matter how busy he was – whether he was marking, going to parents' evenings, doing detentions, or having meetings – he always made time to check up on me outside of class, and that meant more to me than he will ever know.

When you have an illness that makes you feel completely isolated and alone, having a small amount of contact with somebody takes away some of that loneliness. It was like I was drowning in the middle of the sea, and he was in a small boat floating beside me. He couldn't stop me from drowning, but he stood by my side throughout all the pain and suffering so I never felt alone.

CHAPTER 8

HAVE A LIE DOWN

My teachers supported me so much during the hardest year of my school life. I came in to have regular meetings with my Head of Sixth Form, Mr White, as well as Mr Donoghue. My parents would be there too. The meetings often ended up with me breaking down into tears and resting my head on the table, wanting to escape. Mr Donoghue was always able to reassure me and guide me through.

I came back into school just a few times a week. I'd already dropped English, but we soon realised that even continuing with two (biology and Latin) of my three A Levels was too much for me. I couldn't concentrate in lessons, I would cry all the way through break and lunchtimes, and felt completely disconnected from the school environment. In a place where I had excelled and reached my full potential daily for the last six years, I couldn't even deal with one lesson a day. I dropped down to just studying biology, because I had always enjoyed the subject and it genuinely interested me. One of my best friends, Cathy, sat beside me in biology, and she always sensed when I was having a bad day.

My other classmates were all very understanding too. I would be physically present in lessons, but I wouldn't participate or talk to anyone. I couldn't do the practical elements of the lesson either. It was horrendous.

One day during break time I was drinking tea with Mr Donoghue. This is what we usually did if he was on duty. There were rarely, if ever, any incidents that he had to deal with, so it was a good time to chat. We'd sit in the corner in the canteen at a table with a spotted tablecloth. I'd either get myself a tea from the café with my friends and then go and sit with him, or I'd spot him with two polystyrene cups – one with the contents always considerably darker – if he'd already been to the staff room to get them.

On this particular day I spoke to him about how I'd nearly overdosed, how I'd brought the medication into school, and how I was struggling to connect with my friends and peers. He listened, as always, and asked open questions as though he was genuinely interested. He never delved deeper than he needed to. He also never told me he knew how I felt, because he acknowledged that he didn't. I never felt judged. I spoke to him about anything and everything. It was a safe place for me to unload. When the bell went for the end of break – a moment I always dreaded – he had to go to his lesson. I had a free period, which gave my mind too much time to ruminate.

'You gonna be okay?' Mr Donoghue asked as he stacked the cups and put them in the bin. I thought for a moment. I couldn't eally say no, even though that was the truth, because I couldn't stop him from going to his lesson. Besides, I didn't want to worry him.

'Yeah, I'm fine,' I replied, not looking him in the eye.

He walked out of the room and I started thinking about what we'd just discussed. I had been through so much, to the point where I was basically broken. Life was testing me to my absolute limits. I didn't know if I should be in school, and I didn't know what the hell I'd do if I wasn't. It was all I'd ever known for the last 12 years of my life. I never thought I'd be in this situation.

My friend Cathy and I both had a free period, and we usually met to do some work together or have a general chitchat over a cup of tea. Cathy is the best person you'll ever meet. She has the kindest heart and *always* puts others first. She was so supportive during these really tough months where my depression reached its worst. She was there regardless of how I was feeling. I texted her and she found me in that same corner, at that same table with the spotted tablecloth, with my head on the table. My tears had accumulated into little puddles around me.

'Oh, Ruthie,' she said as she wrapped her arms around me in a hug. Cathy gives the best hugs.

'I need to talk to someone,' I told her.

'Do you want me to come with you?' she asked.

'Sure, if that's okay.'

Of course it was okay. She'd do anything to support me. I'm sure she would've even held my hand if we weren't in Year 13 and at risk of getting some strange looks in the corridor.

Most people were in their lessons as we walked through the corridors, which was lucky as I must've looked a mess. I think we were basically just on the hunt for anyone who could offer me an ear for a while. We walked past the Religious Studies office and one of my ex-teachers, Mr Hooper, was sitting alone at his desk, marking some work by the looks of things. Cathy gave me the nod that he would be a good person to talk to. I didn't want her to come with me and she knew that, so she gave me another hug and left me to approach him. Cathy was so great at identifying the right thing to do. I couldn't have been more grateful to have had her by my side.

I knocked on the door and he looked up. I think he was surprised to see me (he had taught me in Year 8, but I hadn't really spoken to him a huge amount since) and assumed that I was going to ask if he knew where one of his colleagues was.

'Hi, Ruth,' he greeted me, smiling. He wore glasses and had a short, dark beard. It was a warm day and his jacket was hanging from the back of his chair.

I stood in the doorway and stumbled through my words. 'Are you free to have a chat?'

'Yeah, of course.' He put his pen down and indicated to a swivel chair next to him.

I was honestly such an emotional mess; I began to cry as soon as I sat down.

I was one of his top students in Year 8. One of the main topics we'd covered was inequality and I regularly brought up the pay gap between male and female footballers. I had brimmed with confidence and loved to voice an opinion especially on something I was so passionate about. I was the girl who played football, and most people knew that.

But all my confidence and passion had trickled away. What must it have been like for him, seeing someone he had previously seen acting strong and independent feeling so powerless and upset?

It was only after 20 minutes that I was actually able to tell him what the issue was. 'It's depression, by the way,' I blurted out as he passed me a box of tissues. I managed to compose myself over the next 10 minutes or so, and he told me how he understood that it was difficult, but it would get better; I was clearly strong enough to fight it. He listened. Midway through our conversation one of his colleagues came into the room. She acknowledged me but didn't say anything. She just went to her desk, which was closest to the door, and started tapping away at her laptop.

It didn't bother me at the time as I was in deep conversation with Mr Hooper, but looking back, it now surprises me that she didn't notice it was a personal conversation. I was very open with everybody about my mental health in Year 13, but others might not have been.

When the bell went for the end of that lesson, I had to decide as to whether I wanted – or felt able – to go to my next lesson which was Latin. I was actually feeling a lot better than when I had first left the canteen after break, and so I was slightly optimistic that I would be able to deal with it.

I stood up and took a deep breath. 'Thank you for taking the time to listen to me, Mr Hooper,' I said. 'I really appreciate it.' I headed towards the door, but the other teacher stopped me at the door. While I'd been talking to Mr Hooper, I'd noticed that she left the room for a phone call. I hadn't thought a nything of it at the time.

'I've just called the school nurse, Ruth,' she said. 'I've told her you're coming to see her.'

Oh God.

My heart dropped to the floor. Tears welled up in my eyes. I felt betrayed. I had told Mr Hooper early on that talking to the nurse just wasn't an option for me as we didn't get on. He'd respected that and allowed me to unload to him as he listened. Now his colleague, who understandably thought this was the right thing to do, had called her without asking me. Looking back, I know now that she had the best intentions.

But at this point I was mortified. If there had been the slightest chance of me going to that Latin lesson, there sure wasn't a chance in hell of that now. I burst into tears and ran.

This is the first time I'd ever actually run to get away from someone in school. I ran past my Latin classroom, where the seats were beginning to fill and where my chair remained empty – where one name on that register would not be ticked. I ran to the toilets and there I stood in a cubicle, feeling gutted. I had no idea what I was meant to do. I wanted to run away. I wanted to escape from school, to escape from the pain, and escape from life.

I didn't understand why I was being forced to see someone who didn't help me. It seemed there was only one procedure for when staff saw a child crying for whatever reason. Bullying? Parents splitting up? Dog dying? Bad test results? Mental illness?

Call the school nurse.

I'm almost certain that she helped a lot of students with their challenges and problems. I'm sure she was good at her job, but in life we can't get on with everyone.

One Friday lunchtime in March I was leaving the canteen and my friends were huddled in the locker area, discussing their plans for the weekend. One was going to Manchester to see her boyfriend, who was a year older and studying at university there. Another was planning to write her English coursework. English coursework I should've been doing. It felt like they all had such ideal lives, and I was just being left behind.

Of course, everyone has their own difficulties to deal with and hurdles to overcome in life, but depression forced me to be selfish and focus solely on my own problems. This, in itself, went against everything I'd ever lived for.

My legs crumbled beneath me and my back slid against the lockers until I was crouching down. I put my head in my hands (an all too familiar position for me at that point) and started crying again. I didn't want to cry in front of my friends, or my peers, or the teachers walking past, but I had no energy left to walk away. I wished I could go to the toilets or go outside, but I was trapped in my own head.

In the corner of my eye I saw one of my teachers. Usually he would ask if I was okay in this situation – and maybe offer to chat – but instead he walked away. It was like a gut-punch; I thought he didn't care, but it was only when Mr White walked around the corner that I realised he had gone to get him.

Mr White is the best Head of Sixth Form in the world. He can flip instantaneously from having a serious phone call with a parent to joking with students in the flick of a switch.

Everyone I knew had the utmost respect for him – I was certainly one of them. I spent more time crying in Mr White's office than I ever thought I would. For someone who had never been to a member of staff's office other than to be commended for academic achievement, it was tough.

'Come on, Ruth, this isn't fair,' he said to me. I felt a surge of anger. Did he think I wanted to be sitting here, bawling my eyes out in front of everyone? Of course I didn't.

In retrospect I now understand what he meant. He was saying that it wasn't fair for me to be struggling there on my own. But it was also unfair to my friends, who were unsure about what to do with me. So he took me outside.

'Can we talk for a little bit?' I asked him. I was fed up, fragile, and vulnerable, but he had guests arriving for a meeting, so he was unable to talk this time.

'I can't just leave you here, though,' he said. 'You need to be with someone. Do you want to see the school nurse?'

I didn't have to say anything. I just gave him a death stare, and that said all I needed to say. Instead he walked me to the medical department, where he passed me over to different school nurse. I had to talk to her, even though this meant explaining my whole back story to her.

I reeled off what I had told every professional so far. I told her about the depression, my injury, my sister going away … I had stopped crying by this point. When I'd finished speaking she had no words other than, 'Do you want to have a lie down on the bed?'

I was so angry at this that steam might as well have been billowing from my ears. A lie down. Of course, that was the answer …

… not!

As the exam period loomed, Mr White and my parents were concerned that I would have limited time to catch up on the work that I'd missed, let alone revise all the material from Year 12 on top of that. And so, in a meeting with my parents in April, I made the tough decision to not take any of my exams that year. Subsequently, I decided not to go to university. I had been predicted two As and one B, and had five offers from top English universities. Just one year ago I'd been considering applying to study medicine. I had been in the top 10 in my year group for all seven years of my school career, and now it seemed I'd lost everything. All that I'd worked for over the course of my time at school had turned to nothing.

I do know now, though, that it was the right decision for me. The school supported me wholeheartedly with it. I think it says a lot about their aims; Mr White reiterated to me several times that health and happiness came before education every time. The school respected that I had a hell of a lot to deal with, without having the stress of exams contributing to it all.

But that didn't stop my personal disappointment. Seeing friends achieving great grades and enjoying the last few weeks of school (this included the highly anticipated Leaver's ball, a highlight of the Sixth Form for many students, which I had felt unable to attend) was very challenging for me. I'd put a lot of pressure on myself to succeed and reach my full potential, a potential which I'd been aware of since infant school.

Depression had stopped me from doing that, and it frustrated me. A lot.

I continued to talk to Mr Donoghue and other teachers on a regular basis. He helped me to believe in myself, to remind me that I was stronger than my demons, and that I had got through it before. But without medication or continuous and reliable support from services, it was incredibly difficult to see the light or any future at all.

Two days after my 18th birthday, I received a letter in the post from CAMHS saying that they could no longer support me due to my age. This was despite telling me that they would finish their treatment with me before this happened. I received no referral to adult services, so I was left out of the system. My parents didn't ever talk to me about how any of this felt for them, and I had no idea how they felt about it. They reacted in the same way to a lot of things. I think it was just easier for us all to avoid talking about how we felt.

I moved further and further away from them emotionally. Not only did I not want to hurt them, but I also didn't want to be misunderstood by them either. I was protecting them as well as myself.

CHAPTER 9

THE CALM BEFORE THE STORM

Time and emotional support eventually did the job that CAMHS had not.

With Mr Donoghue's help, I began feeling more positive over time. We both saw improvements. Gradually things got better and I developed a different demeanour. My shoulders were no longer tense; I became more confident and bubbly. I started to look to the future and laughed more. I found I could join in with childish banter, something that had seemed impossible for me a few weeks before. I imagine it was rewarding for Mr Donoghue to see. He'd sat with me at my lowest points – when I'd been at my most vulnerable – and yet he chose to stick by my side regardless. It really says a lot about someone's character when they are willing to stand by your side in the darkness. He supported me until I was at a stage where I was more stable, content, and confident.

I left school in mid-June with very mixed feelings. I felt like a failure in a way. It had never crossed my mind that I'd be unable to finish my A Levels, and I was unsure of what my future held for me. I knew that I'd come a long way though, and that the skills I'd acquired through the tough times were incomparable to A Level certificates. My determination and resilience had helped me through.

And I'd made an impact on people, which is all I ever aspire to do.

On my last day of school, my Latin teacher, Miss Newton, approached me in the corridor. I'd always looked up to her and admired her enormously; she was an incredibly strong woman and always held her ground. She'd taught me for four years and had an infectious passion for the subject she taught. We'd always got on well. I'd achieved an A in my AS Level in Year 12, so I was on track to achieve the same in Year 13. For this reason it pained me to let her down, as she had done such an amazing job in teaching us.

As she stood next to me in that corridor, the age gap became meaningless, as did our roles as student and teacher. We were two strong, independent women who I felt had been slightly battered by life, but here we stood tall together. 'You just never know who you're inspiring, Ruth,' she told me. 'You inspired me when I taught you.'

I didn't ever think teachers were inspired by their students. I smiled at her and blinked back tears of gratitude. So many of my teachers have inspired me and have helped mould me into who I am today, so to hear this from her meant an awful lot.

Throughout that summer I was all too aware that I hadn't had the ongoing psychological support that I needed. Therefore, my thought patterns hadn't completely changed, so a part of me still doubted and shot down anything positive that happened. Despite this, I put on a brave and happy face throughout much of the uncertainty.

I wanted to take my football to the next level, to use it as a vehicle to drive me forward. I needed something to focus my attention. I was in a confused place; I was training with lots of different personal trainers and trying different diets. I was genuinely a bit lost, unsure of what I was doing or trying to achieve.

Eventually I was approached by Dylan Logan, the brother of Hugo, the young MK Dons player. He had struggled with multiple injuries and suffered mentally because of this. He was trained by a guy called Steve Linger, a strength coach who specialises in functioning and moving correctly. I looked him up on Instagram and was amazed by his work. He trained the best – from semi-pro to fully professional footballers – as well as people from various other backgrounds.

I liked what I saw and pinged him a message. He replied and we booked in a first session – which I bailed on. I told him I needed to cover a colleague's shift at work, which was complete rubbish. Quite honestly, I was scared that he was too good for me, that I was too weak-minded because mentally I was still in a very bad place.

So, we rearranged. And I bailed again. This time I blamed a minor hip strain. After a third cancellation, this time blaming my financial situation, he started to pry gently, asking if there was anything else going on. I told him I had a story if he wanted to hear it, and he invited me to send it over.

Wow, he replied. *That must've been tough to put all that down on paper. Get your arse in the gym soon and let's make your dream, your passion, which is quite clearly football, a reality.*

When I finally made it into the gym, I was scared and timid. I was concerned that because I'd opened up to him about my depression, he would look at me in a different light. But I couldn't have been more wrong – he saw me as a footballer and only a footballer. We set out a plan, looking at how he was going to help me.

One of his top clients, a Watford Ladies player who had just recovered from an anterior cruciate ligament injury, had a partner called Sean who was a coach at Cambridge United Women's Football Club. After several weeks of training with Steve, eliminating the minor niggles that had been holding me back, I signed for Cambridge.

It was a huge step up for me. I'd gone from Second Division county-level football to Women's Premier League level in the space of a few weeks. But I loved the challenge.

I corresponded with Kevin, the Chair of the club and the first team manager. I needed to talk to him about the troubled year I'd had, and I wanted to tell him that depression was still eating away at my insides. As it turned out, he was on holiday when I messaged him asking if I could talk to him. That wasn't ideal, as it was often better to talk in person about these issues. I did tell him though, and he reassured me that the club had my back. They would support me in any way they could, and I appreciated that a lot.

Towards the back end of summer I made a surprising, spontaneous decision: to go to the University of Hertfordshire to study a foundation degree course in Sports Studies. As it turned out, my AS Level grades from Year 12 allowed me to do this. Leaving home would give me the independence that I so needed. I couldn't deal with the tension at home anymore. My parents were struggling to deal with my illness, and I was fed up of coming across as rude or ungrateful, but I didn't want to let them in. I didn't want them to know what I was doing and I especially didn't want them to know how I was feeling.

I hoped I could start again with a clean slate, where depression wouldn't be the defining part of my life and where people didn't know about my past.

The first three weeks were really positive. I was able to be the real Ruth Fox, who had been lost for so long. I got drunk, began to excel in my studies again, and made a lot of new friends. I was playing for the university women's football first team and enjoying it all.

It felt like I had been miraculously cured from depression once again, but in reality, this was all just a distraction. It was the calm before the storm.

CHAPTER 10

A FRESH START?

I always knew I'd go to university. The typical route of education for most young people was GCSEs at school, A Levels in college or Sixth Form, and a degree at university before starting a career. This was especially true for those attending a private school. Other options (BTECs, scholarships abroad, and apprenticeships) were never really discussed a huge amount but that didn't bother me. I thought I had my path set up and my plan was sorted.

And so, when the opportunity arose for me to go to the University of Hertfordshire to study Sports Studies, I grasped hold of it with both hands. I needed to get away from home.

One night – I think it was day three of Freshers' Week (the first week of the university term) – my housemate, Matt, and I decided to go out. We went to Tesco to get the necessary beverages to get us slightly drunk before we went out (okay, when I say "slightly" drunk ...). I think we spent £30 on a mixture of cheap spirits, beer, and mixers. We brought them back to the house, and it was literally just the both of us in the kitchen. I plugged my music into my speaker and just let my hair down.

I wanted to be a different person, just for a few hours. I was done with being judged by other people – or rather, *thinking* I was being judged by other people. I just wanted the black cloud to dissipate from above my head. I wanted to be the Ruthie I was before my diagnosis four years before.

Fuck that doctor, I thought in my drunken state. *Why did he have to diagnose me with depression?*

We stumbled to the shuttle bus stop and waited for the bus to take us to the other campus, where the party would begin. It took an age to arrive, so we decided to walk as it was only a mile or so. We continued to drink as we walked and we met a lovely group of flatmates who we bonded with immediately.

I started to feel that comforting buzz that alcohol gives you. I loved the feeling. I introduced myself to each member of the group individually, and soon I became a popular member of it. Soon we were already exchanging numbers and planning more nights out together.

The rest of the night is a bit of a blur if I'm honest. I remember buying drink after drink after drink. As soon as one was finished, I was up at the bar again. The music was running through my veins and filling me with an elixir of life. I was in heaven. What the fuck was depression?

One third year student tried it on with me. I asked him to buy me a drink (I don't know where this confidence came from) and he did. After that I said, 'I'm just going to the loo,' and then I abandoned him. I didn't need a man in my life. I was enjoying my own company and the company of my new friends.

The club closed at 2.00am. After being chatted up by two more guys I made an exit with Matt. We jumped on the shuttle bus and headed back to our new buddies' flat. I remember taking straight shots of vodka while working my way through sickly sweet cider. I didn't want this night to end.

Matt stayed and chilled with us for a while and then went home. I headed out with someone else (I have no idea who) and went over to another flat on campus. I danced around their kitchen, ate their nachos, and tried to prolong the night as much as I could. Reality scared me so much. I enjoyed this drunk dreamworld.

As I finished my next Kopparberg, I realised I had had one too many. I lay my head on the kitchen bar and blacked out for a few seconds. The next thing I knew, one of the girls was calling Matt to come and collect me. I felt bad that he had to come out to get me, like I was his child, and he was picking me up from a party. When he arrived I gave him a huge hug as though he was my dad, and then we set off walking very slowly back to our house.

I was so out of it. I needed to stop every few minutes, sometimes just to make some "hilarious" comment about our surroundings, sometimes just to take a breather. I stopped on a grass verge next to the road in between uni and our house (although at the time I genuinely thought we were still miles away from home) and just sat there for a while. I have no idea how long for.

Matt was getting concerned. 'Shall we go now, Ruth? We're nearly home.'

As soon as I heard his words, my throat started closing up. I gasped for air. I could feel every single heartbeat in my chest. It was one of the scariest moments of my life. I put my head between my legs ...

... and then there was a black nothingness ...

When I opened my eyes, there were bright flashing lights. I covered them with my hands, feeling the presence of someone beside me. I could hear two male voices and I jumped.

I realised that it was Matt, accompanied by a paramedic who was dressed in green. I relaxed a bit. He asked me if I was okay, but I was still breathing really quickly. I struggled to control it long enough to answer him.

'Take your time, Ruth,' said the paramedic. 'Nice and easy. In and out.'

My head was spinning, probably from the vast amount of alcohol I'd drunk that night. What had I done? I was regretting everything.

'How much have you had to drink?' the paramedic asked me.

'A lot.' Incredibly accurate.

'Any mental health issues?' he asked, not even batting an eyelid.

'Yes, depression,' I replied, although I didn't know what that had to do with it.

But maybe it did. Had I drunk copious amounts of alcohol to become a depression-less Ruth for just a night? Had I been trying to find a girl who had been lost for well over six months? Had I subconsciously turned to drink for solace, or was I just being a classic student? I'm not sure.

The paramedic began to take my blood pressure but was struggling to get any reliable readings. 'Looks like we're going to have to take you to the hospital, Ruth,' he said. Well, this was a new experience, going in a paramedic's car. He and Matt helped me to my feet as I wobbled all over the place. With some effort, I was helped into the car.

The hospital was about 20 miles away. On our way there, blue lights and all, I learnt that the paramedic's name was Rob. He spoke to me and I kind of opened up to him about the terrible year I'd had. I told him I wasn't even supposed to have gone to university, that I hadn't finished my A Levels. I didn't care that Matt was in the back of the car. I just needed to let it out.

Rob was really relaxed about it all, despite me bawling my eyes out. 'Have you ever had a panic attack before?' he asked.

'No.'

'Well, not until today,' he said.

We arrived at the hospital and the paramedic spoke with the receptionist, who told me to take a seat in the waiting area. I drank a good litre of water from the tepid water machine while I was waiting, trying to sober up just a little so that I wouldn't look entirely like a drunken mess. I was repping my university with their sports hoody, so I don't think I was doing them – or me – any favours. I imagined the other patients thinking, *Oh, there's another drunken student on a Saturday night, using up our resources.*

After 20 minutes (note how much quicker this was than when I went to A&E for self harm earlier in the year ...) my name was called out, and I was led behind a curtain where I was made to lie down. There they took my blood pressure. The nurse looked at me as though I had just been stupid, which I clearly had been. But I didn't need her scowling at me, reminding me of it.

I was given the all-clear and sent on my way. Matt called a taxi for us and paid for it. There was silence on the way home.

I was genuinely so scared of turning to alcohol as a coping mechanism, that I stopped drinking from that point onwards. I haven't touched alcohol since.

Three weeks into university I found myself alone with my thoughts again. That thick, black cloud, which was becoming all too frequent in my life, began to overshadow everything again. This time I sought help quickly, aware of how serious things could get. I went to the university GP, who concluded that I had serious depression and moderate anxiety. He prescribed fluoxetine at 10 mg a day. He also referred me to the University wellbeing services, where I had one appointment with a lady who was heavily pregnant. Despite opening up to her about self-harming in an assessment, I wasn't passed onto anyone else when she immediately went on maternity leave.

Fluoxetine was both my best friend and my worst enemy. And unfortunately, it proved to be more of the latter once again. Suicidal thoughts clouded my head and I had vivid visualisations of overdosing on the bottle of fluoxetine every day. I was self-harming daily, and soon my wrists, ribs, shoulders, and hips were covered in scars. Cutting became part of my everyday routine.

It was here at university that my eating disorder flared up again. I had money and was alone much of the time. I would eat a lot. I'd sit there slitting my wrists (or hips, or ribs) while munching on a packet of chocolate digestives, a box of popcorn, and a bag of Haribo. I'd do this while waiting for a Domino's pizza, then attempt to burn it off in the gym at 6.00am the following morning. It wasn't good at all.

I must've gained quite a bit of weight at uni, but because I naturally have a broad body shape (except for when I weigh 40kg) it wasn't that obvious. I think obesity levels in the UK – and in fact the world – are an indication of the state of society's mental health. Comfort eating (whether that's followed by guilt or satisfaction, it doesn't matter) is a coping mechanism. Eating feels good for most people, and it's something we can control in our lives. I had two very different experiences of food throughout my bouts of depression, and I don't think that's a coincidence. Changes in weight are often symptoms of depression and other mental illnesses.

One really tough day I told my friend that I didn't feel safe leaving her. We went to A&E together to seek help, as recommended once again when we called NHS 111. It was another Saturday night, at around 7.00pm. By the time I was seen, dozens of patients had come and gone. I was clearly very stressed, prowling the waiting area like a tiger in a zoo. I was desperate for someone to help me. There were two police officers supervising some drunks and I was so tempted to talk to them. I just needed help from someone; I was literally crying out.

After a seemingly endless seven hours of waiting, I was seen by the mental health team. There was a more senior man in trousers and an unbuttoned shirt and a young man with jeans, a t-shirt and a lanyard around his neck. They looked very stressed. The older man was red-faced and sweating. The young guy held a clipboard and seemed to take control.

I broke down immediately. Being there was very daunting. I was completely and utterly fed up with this illness, and the way it dictated my life.

'Would you like ten minutes to sit outside and compose yourself?' the younger nurse asked.

Was he joking?

I sighed and took a long, deep breath, to make sure I was calm enough not to shout at him. 'I've been waiting for seven hours,' I said. 'I'm not waiting for any longer.'

I explained to them exactly how I felt as honestly as I could. It took a lot of guts for me to lay it all out there on the table. But their response disappointed me.

'You do realise that that amount of fluoxetine won't kill you, you know. If that's what you're trying to achieve,' the older guy said smugly. He sat back in his chair as if he was incredibly powerful, looking down at me. I felt intimidated.

'We can't give you any answers, Ruth,' the younger man continued. 'You're going to have to come up with those yourself. If you think you are going to overdose on this medication, what could you do to stop yourself?'

I thought for a bit. 'I guess I can give it to my friend,' I answered quietly. She was waiting outside.

This idea seemed adequate enough for them, and they sent me on my way with no referral to any mental health services or crisis teams. I was angry. I was really quite scared of what I would do to myself. I'd come here to get their help. I needed help!

I wouldn't have waited for seven hours if I didn't believe this! And yet I left in the same situation I had been in when I'd arrived.

It put such a lot of pressure on my friend, and this had only distracted me from the problem instead of helping me to solve it.

I got into my bed at 4.00am that morning, having spent £30 on a taxi getting home. I was disappointed and let down. A few hours after I'd genuinely contemplated ending it all, I still had no ongoing support and I still felt unsafe. Surely a referral to a crisis team was a necessity?

I had a football game at 2.00pm the same day. I knew I needed to play to relieve some of that anguish and pain.

CHAPTER 11

GAME DAY

Game day starts the minute you wake up. As the sunlight seeps through the curtains, a wave of excitement, intertwined with nerves and expectation, washes over me. I become focused only on the task at hand.

When my tracksuit is on and breakfast is demolished, I throw my bag into the boot and get into the car. This is when I am transformed from the struggling, timid teenager to an experienced athlete. With the music blaring from the radio and a strong coffee in my hand, I fully prepare myself for the game.

Today was the perfect weather for a football match. The breeze wafted through my hair and it was surprisingly warm for a Sunday in mid-winter. As I pulled up at the ground, I took a moment to admire the pitch – a carpet of lush greenness, and at the same time a battle ground, a boxing ring. I couldn't wait to be where I felt most comfortable in the world.

It didn't matter to me who the opposition was or who I was playing for, or whether it was a cup game, a league game, a five-a-side charity match, or a training match. Whatever it was, I knew it was my time to be myself. In a world of darkness, where all I could do was fight the thoughts in my own head, here was my safe place. I no longer wanted to end my own life or harm myself. Here I could channel those emotions and forget about everything else.

I was a changed person when I got out of the car. To my teammates it seemed like I was bouncing off the walls, full of banter and laughter. Little did they know that a few hours previously I'd been battling suicidal thoughts in A&E.

Rooted inside me is a deep focus, an urge to perform at my best. I have to win. Nothing else is good enough.

I sat in the changing rooms, visualising the game and my role within it. I thought about the objectives we'd worked on in training. This particular week it was dropping off, being an option, receiving from one side and switching play with a long ping into the corner for a winger to run onto. I was excited to put this into action.

I tied up my boots and put on my shirt. I had a complete mindset that would help me to succeed. Yes, I had doubts, of course I did. Every day I doubt myself and my ability. I don't think I'm good enough, and I don't think I ever will be. But it doesn't stop me putting 100 per cent into everything I do.

While the girls were finishing getting changed, I went and had a chat with Kevin, who was setting up the warm-up outside. He was putting a cone down when I approached him.

'Hi mate, everything okay?' he asked.

I told him everything that had happened the night before – how frustrated I was, how vulnerable I felt, how hard I was fighting every single day. I didn't want depression to take football away from me.

He didn't say much. He just stood and listened to me with attention and respect. 'We'll take it minute by minute,' he said. 'You don't have to play if you don't want to.'

Feeling reassured, I started to warm up. Here I'm able to have a ball at my feet, to get touches, to feel relaxed and at home.

I stretched off any niggling aches and pains, but ultimately I was just counting down until I heard that whistle.

Whenever the referee puts the whistle to his lips and the game commences, I immediately want to be on the ball. I've played too many games in my career to know that I have a tendency to give too much too soon. I can get over-excited, miss my first tackle, take a heavy touch, or try something too risky too early on. So as soon as I receive the ball, I take a breath, look up, lay it off to the right back, and get on the move again. Here I am in my happy place. I'm always learning, always progressing.

My first opportunity to switch the ball came. I received it on my back foot and swung at it. I didn't put enough on it and the ball got cut off by the opposition's left-back. She powered forward, nipping in front of our winger and taking back possession. I jumped on the spot, writhing inside, feeling frustrated. But no one stopped to pat me on the back and say, 'Don't worry, better luck next time.' Of course they didn't. This was a game of football. We make mistakes, we get up, we try again. There's no time to mull things over.

There were a few opportunities within the game. The opposition was technically weak but worked hard. We had a corner midway through the first half. I am a keen header of the ball, an unusual attribute in the women's game (although this is improving). My teammate teed up the ball as I lost my marker by making darting runs. She couldn't be bothered to stay with me because she didn't think I was dangerous.

As the ball swung in from the left, curving towards the goal, I sprinted towards it. I was determined to get there, and I did before anyone else. The ball hit a part of my body – possibly my shoulder or the side of my head – but it didn't matter. The ball was in the net.

There is no feeling in the world more satisfying than scoring a goal. The only way I can describe this feeling is like getting a "power up" when playing a game. It feels like you have more oxygen going to your muscles, more air in your lungs, more endorphins flowing through your body. There really is no other feeling like it.

I jogged over to the player who took the corner: it was a perfect delivery. Other teammates high-fived me as I ran back, ready to restart.

When half time came about, we were level at 1–1. We had switched off once we had scored and allowed a through ball to cut through our defence, onto a pacey forward to run onto. The dressing room was bubbling with tension, excitement, and frustration … but I was quiet. I was focused. I listened to what the manager had to say about the parts of our game we needed to work on, the bits we were doing well. I listened and I took it in. But I also had an idea of what I needed to work on individually.

Walking out after half time, we knew it was make or break. We had 45 minutes to make a difference.

The remainder of the game was disjointed. The ball ping-ponged around. I won several headers in the heart of midfield, jumping to compete but giving away a few fouls along the way. I had another chance to switch the ball. Our left-back had the ball, so I checked my shoulders and called for it, indicating that I wanted the ball to be played just in front of me. I took a touch and then another, driving forward up the pitch. I looked up again, making eye contact with our right winger who had begun a strong run down the line. I took one more touch to push the ball away from my feet and struck it sweetly.

You can tell from the feeling – and also the spin of the ball on its axis – that it has been hit well. The ball landed a few yards in front of our right winger, ready for her to pick it up and continue with the attack. The ball she delivered was overhit and ended up going out for a goal kick. But that was okay. It was a good move.

As I jogged back into position I heard my coach call my name. I looked up, but he didn't say anything more. He just raised his hands and applauded me. I knew I had done the right thing and that I'd be rewarded.

As the game drew in it became tense. But then an opportunity just like the one before came up. This time I dropped off, got the ball from our left winger, took one touch, and pinged it in the opposite direction. I could do this move in my sleep now, it felt so natural. The ball landed perfectly on the diagonal, and the right winger took one touch and thumped it home into the top left corner. Job done. 2–1.

When the final whistle came, I was disappointed that the game had come to an end. I was aware that as soon as I got back in my car to drive home, my thoughts would overpower my mind again. I would struggle on, fighting every minute of every day.

My release was over ... until next week.

CHAPTER 12

LET DOWN, AGAIN

I had made my university football coach aware of my previous problems, so initially I could turn to him. Staff from both the university and the football team were becoming increasingly concerned about my wellbeing and the lack of support I was getting. So, following several emails from lecturers and coaches, I had an appointment with the Head of Mental Health at the university, three weeks after I had personally emailed him asking for an appointment, again asking for help. It lasted for an hour and a half, and I had never spoken so bluntly in my life. I told him I didn't feel safe leaving that room, which was the honest truth. I felt a strange comfort in that room, like I couldn't deal with the reality beyond those four walls. Alarmed, he arranged for a taxi to take me to see the community mental health crisis team in the next town.

Following yet another assessment there, I was told the crisis team would come to my house every day to support me and check that I was okay. They also decided to take me off the fluoxetine, concluding that it had contributed to my suicidal thoughts and visions.

I kept my coach updated throughout the day as I was due to play in a match that afternoon. I managed to get a taxi back following my appointment and play the second half for the university team. For 45 minutes I completely forgot about everything.

The crisis team gave me a two-hour window during which they'd visit. The first day they were due to arrive between 10.00am and 12.00 noon. But then I got a phone call at 12.09pm saying they'd be there between 3.00pm and 5.00pm. I was incredibly anxious and on edge, and I struggled to believe that they would keep their word. Being a university student living in shared accommodation, I had to make sure none of my house mates were in the kitchen during these times, so changing arrangements just made things even harder. What also didn't help was that every day a different person came, meaning I couldn't build a relationship or rapport with any one individual. It felt like I was just being ticked off a list. One day I put my head on the table, upset, and when I looked up the crisis team worker who had been beside me just left without even telling me. That's how I felt ... alone and let down.

I became more and more withdrawn every day.

The Sunday of that week was one of the hardest days. They didn't send anyone out to me because a limited number of people worked on a Sunday and I wasn't on the high priority list. Clearly mental ill health is only a Monday to Friday, 9–5pm issue. They were meant to call me, just to check in, but unsurprisingly that never happened.

I was meant to have a football game for my club in the afternoon, and I wanted to go because football was my only release. And yet, when I tried to get in the car to travel on three separate occasions, I just couldn't do it. I couldn't deal with the pressure, the people ... anything.

I was letting my teammates and my coach down. Without football, I'd have nothing. My mental illness was taking my whole life away from me: my friends, my family, my studies, and my football. I spent that whole day in a coffee shop near where I lived, composing myself and thinking.

When I finally went back home, I couldn't find anywhere to park. I became more and more stressed, and my anxiety was building by the second. I had to reverse into a tight space and managed to brush the car behind me. No one was hurt, and neither car suffered from any damage at all, but this was the straw that broke the camel's back. I sped off to Tesco car park, the only place I knew would be quiet as it was after closing time. I was breathing heavily and crying uncontrollably.

I knew I needed help. I had bought three whole packets of paracetamol a few days before, and I was certain, should I go home, I would take them all. I didn't want to hurt myself, but I saw no way out.

I texted one of my coaches, Sean, as I had no idea what I was meant to do. He said I should call an ambulance. I'd never called any of the emergency services before and I thought it was wrong to call one for yourself.

No, it's fine, Sean wrote. *It shows that you understand you need help.*

I didn't see any other options, so I called. The lady on the other end of the line said they couldn't send anyone out as they were too busy, but they'd get a clinician to call me within two hours. And so once again I was left on my own, expected to just sit in my car in Tesco car park at 11.00pm, waiting for a phone call that I feared would never come.

I waited. And waited. After a while it became too much. Two hours came and went. No one called me. I got out of my car and walked to the road.

Would jumping in front of a car mean certain death? I wondered. *Or would it just cause me short or long-term damage? Would the driver get hurt? What speed were the cars driving at?*

What the hell do I need to do to get the help I'm crying out for?

My reality became distorted; thoughts were travelling through my mind at a million miles an hour. Several people walked past me, but no one stopped to check that I was okay. It didn't matter. I clearly wasn't worthy.

I stood by that road in the freezing cold darkness for over an hour. My family had no idea I was in this situation. I had hidden everything from them. I never went back to visit them at all; I barely replied to their messages. I just put it down to being so busy with my new life at university. In reality, I was in a place darker than they could ever have imagined.

Exhausted, defeated, I made the decision to drive home. I was too tired to do anything but sleep when I got in. The thought of the paracetamol tablets I'd bought mocked and tormented me until I drifted off to sleep, fully clothed. But my moment of peace was interrupted by a call at 5.00am from a private number.

I assumed this was the ambulance. I didn't pick it up.

They had called me six hours after I had cried out for help. Anything could've happened to me during that time. I was so angry and sick of being messed about all the time.

Luckily for me, a doctor from the crisis team was due to see me the following morning. She was the first professional I had come across who understood me instantly. I explained all of the events from the night before and she listened with no judgement (a recurring essential skill possessed by those who had the most impact on me in this journey). She gave me some promethazine (an antihistamine and sedative) to take the edge off things and calm me down when things got too much. She also referred me to an Acute Day Treatment Unit at the local hospital, the same hospital I had been born in some 18 years before. I don't know why but I found this somewhat ironic. It made me feel like I'd failed at life and was being sent back to the beginning.

This was just one step before getting admitted as an inpatient. I didn't really know what to expect. I was very scared.

I knew I was unwell, but I didn't think I was that unwell.

CHAPTER 13

MY EXPERIENCE IN HOSPITAL

Hospital transport picked me up daily at around 8.30am. The driver, Iain, was one of the nicest men I've ever met. He was middle-aged, fairly tall, with mousy-brown hair and had a slight lisp. He laughed a lot and was just generally incredibly bubbly. His cheeriness was infectious and he made me feel at ease. He treated all of his passengers with respect, as though we were no different from anyone else. And that's exactly how it should be. For some reason, though, I still assumed he thought we were all mad. I certainly thought I was.

'How are you doing, Ruth?' he asked me the first morning.

'Not great. I haven't had a coffee yet,' I replied. I'd missed my alarm.

He chuckled. 'We can stop here if you want,' he said, pointing towards a nearby Shell garage. 'We're going to be early anyway.'

'Do you not think I'll run away if you let me out of the van?' I asked.

'You wouldn't have answered the door to me or got yourself into the van if you wanted to run away,' he smiled. He trusted me, and it put me at ease. I really felt I could talk to Iain – not about what I'd been through (he made a point not to pry), but about life. We talked about his life and his kids. I really enjoyed learning about him. It was such a relief to not be at the centre of attention the whole time. He was just one of those all-round good eggs. I was grateful to have met him. He probably had the biggest impact on me during my hospital visit.

When we pulled up at the hospital on my first day, I was met by a support worker who showed me around. The building was situated right next to the inpatient Mental Health Unit. The doors were automatic, which genuinely surprised me. Did we not need to be locked in? What if we ran away?

There was a kitchen where we could make tea and (decaf only) coffee. It struck me that there were no metal knives, forks, or spoons. There were locks on the drawers and no mugs or plates. Everything was white and smelt like disinfectant, an overwhelming reminder that this was a hospital. There was a lounge area with a small pool table, a brimming bookshelf, and an arrangement of armchairs, which reminded me of an old people's home. There were colouring books and jigsaws piled up. A TV in one corner that seemed to be always tuned into BBC Radio 2. To the left of the lounge there was the medical room, where a nurse was filing through documents and boxes of medication.

Along one side of the main corridor there were five rooms which were for individual appointments. The support worker led me into one of these rooms and closed the door. She smiled and spoke to me about how things worked here. I was incredibly overwhelmed and it felt too much, like I was a fraud.

I shouldn't be here.

After an assessment with the doctor I was prescribed mirtazapine, an antidepressant. They then undertook physical tests, which included an ECG, urine test, blood tests, blood pressure, temperature, and BMI. I met with the other patients too. There were such a variety of ages, characters, and illnesses. One lady had manic depression. Often she would be as high as a kite, laughing and hugging people, but she also had periods where she would become frantic and depressed. It was hard to watch. She asked God to help her through her illness. Unfortunately, over the next few weeks she would become an inpatient. Her husband was unable to look after her at home and she was rapidly deteriorating. It was hard to see.

Another lady had severe obsessive compulsive disorder (OCD) and anxiety. She would ask at least a dozen times an hour for her medication, even though it was given to the patients at the same time (3.00pm) every day. She constantly asked if she was on fire, if she smelt bad, if she was dressed. She was clearly so confused; I just wished I could help in some way. Over the next few weeks I often took her to the Costa coffee shop in the main hospital, just beyond the maternity unit. We'd go to get her a sandwich and give her a change of scenery. I hoped that this gave her just a little bit of relief.

I spoke in-depth to a man who had been in the royal navy for six and a half years. He'd spent 18 years at MI5 and three years in the SAS. He suffered horrendously from post-traumatic stress disorder (PTSD) and had tried to take his own life on three occasions. He told me he couldn't talk to me about the flashbacks or the nightmares he had, because he was worried it would have a negative effect on me.

There were two younger women too, both about 20 years old. I got on really well with them. They'd both struggled with psychotic episodes and had been inpatients previously, one having been to this particular unit at least six times before.

I spent three weeks at the hospital. The staff were lovely, especially Steve, one of the nurses. I played pool with him regularly and we spoke about football a lot. He was from the same area of Yorkshire as my mum.

One of the nurses who was there for just one day was in fact the same young man who had seen me at A&E that night at uni, the one who held the clipboard.

'Do you remember me from A&E?' I asked him, trying to hold back my anger. If he'd done something to help me that night, maybe I wouldn't have ended up here in the first place. I'd gone there, and waited seven hours, for help and they'd had an opportunity to intervene, to refer me to services. But instead I had reached crisis point (as so many of us do) before getting the help I needed.

'I do, yes,' he said, looking sheepish. It frustrates me even now to write this.

My days consisted of therapy sessions, creative sessions, cooking, games, and socialising. We all had our good and bad days. Someone said to me one day that I shouldn't be there because I was too happy. I was frustrated. Why was there this ideal image of a suicidal or depressed person that we all had to live up to? I seemed to be a positive person on the outside, and I tried to make the other patients' lives a little bit more bearable. I hid my own feelings a lot.

I had powerful demons that I had to fight daily, and being in hospital didn't take any of that away. One evening back at University, I reached rock bottom again. I still had the three packets of paracetamol in my room, as well as the 11 mirtazapine tablets I had recently been prescribed. I laid on my bed for hours and hours on my stomach, fixated on the idea of taking them all. I didn't want anyone to find me so much so that I locked my bedroom door. I just wanted complete nothingness, respite from this horrendous illness.

I reached for the packet of mirtazapine and slipped all 11 into my mouth, one at a time. I took a swig of water with each one.

Time for the pain to end.

And yet, once I'd finished the packet, I stopped myself. There were still three packs of paracetamol sitting in front of me, but I couldn't go any further. I can't ever really describe how much mental strength that took, but somehow I got through it. I slept away the guilt and frustration.

The following day I had a day off from hospital, but I rang them up and said I'd had a rough night, so it was probably best that I came in. I sat down and spoke to my psychologist and support worker about the events of the night before. They listened and didn't judge at all. I imagine they'd heard much worse to be honest. They commended my strength and my decision to be straight with them.

A nurse then decided to take me off mirtazapine. She didn't start me on any new medication. I handed in the paracetamol so I could sleep easy at night.

I was at hospital at the weekends as well as during the week, which meant I was unable to play football games for my club or university. I missed it tremendously. I kept myself going by kicking a ball around the garden.

To be honest, I felt like a caged animal in the hospital. I wanted to be outside doing things, being with my friends, studying, and playing football. I was missing out on life. I was weak and powerless, and I hated that feeling. And despite my previous desperation and my cries for help, I still found it difficult to accept that I actually needed it.

Following my overdose and a review appointment, my doctor discussed diagnosing me with bipolar depression. In their literature, the Depression and Bipolar Support Alliance states that:

The symptoms of unipolar depression and bipolar depression are very similar. The main difference is that someone with unipolar depression doesn't experience the highs periods of mania (if severe) or hypomania (if mild). And this is extremely important, because the preferred treatments of the two can be quite different.

I was given this diagnosis because, I was told, I had periods of extreme lows followed by manic highs. I really don't agree with this diagnosis at all because I never had any manic highs. I would sometimes (as in once a week) get hyper because one of my friends in the hospital and I would laugh hysterically. This wasn't mania; this was just me trying to bring back part of the old Ruth that I missed. This was just a release from the darkness constantly overpowering my head.

Clinically depressed people can laugh. It doesn't mean they suffer from bipolar disorder.

The doctor brought up the possibility of putting me on a mood stabiliser such as quetiapine, to help level out my emotions. This is an antipsychotic drug . However, my discharge came too soon and in my discharge meeting we discussed passing on my medication to the outpatient team. I still felt suicidal, no one ever asked me directly whether I was feeling like this though. I didn't feel that being in the hospital environment was helping me in any way at all. It was insightful when other patients talked about their past experiences, but it was also triggering.

Lauren was the care coordinator allocated to me. A care coordinator overlooks treatment following hospital discharge. She was one of those wishy-washy people who never made concrete plans and always seemed distracted. My initial appointment following discharge was supposed to be within seven days, but she didn't make contact until the eighth.

'Why didn't you make your appointment, Ruth?' she asked me on the phone.

'Sorry, what?' I replied, confused.

'You had an appointment today at 3.00pm.'

I was gobsmacked. 'You literally have never told me this,' I told her truthfully.

Just great. I was already on the back foot.

I dropped everything (including a football match for the university) to attend a rearranged appointment at 2.30pm the following day. When I got there, I was met with a delightful greeting.

'I didn't think you were coming.'

I looked at my watch. I was 10 minutes early. 'Why's that?' I asked.

'Your appointment was for 2.00pm.'

Argh. We 100 per cent did not say 2.00pm. We said 2.30pm!

Despite the fact that the communication was lacking on her part, it felt like everything was my fault. And then when Lauren was off sick for two weeks, I was left with no contact and no goal to reach. I just clung on, taking life minute by minute and nothing more.

The hope – for me especially – was for me to be integrated back into university. I wanted to be back with my friends; I wanted to play football, stay independent, and study.

Ideally I needed a meeting with both the hospital and the university to organise a plan, so that we could figure out how they could best support me. But neither organisation were prepared to have external meetings, therefore, the responsibility of finding a way forward, as it so often had been, was placed on my tender shoulders.

CHAPTER 14

'YOU'VE BEEN DISCHARGED. EVERYTHING MUST BE OKAY.'

I ended up having two meetings with my course leader and the head of safeguarding at the university, who I'd never met before. They made the decision that they didn't have the resources to support me, so I had to defer until the following year. Despite feeling that this was potentially the right decision for me, I would've liked to have had a say in it. I was suddenly left to fend entirely for myself. This meant sorting out all the financial implications of deferring my place; loans, rent, bills, accommodation, As a side note, I had to continue paying all my rent and bills for the whole year, which felt entirely unfair and out of order considering this was a medical reason for leaving, and it wasn't even mine!

I had to go back and live at home. That was always going to be a challenge. I had to try to rebuild my life brick by brick.

I noticed that my discharge letter, which I had received a few days after I'd left the hospital, stated that I'd also been diagnosed with adjustment disorder. I didn't even know what this was. I'd never heard of it. None of the professionals working with me had ever mentioned it to me, so nothing was done to help me deal with it. In the letter they had ticked the box "No" to the question "Is the patient aware of their diagnosis?" It still stumps me now. How was I ever meant to even try to get better if I didn't even know what the issue was? The other diagnosis given to me were "emotional issues" and "history of depression", which to me sounded vague and spotlight that they didn't really have any understanding of what was going on with me.

I have now found out that an adjustment disorder is an excessive reaction to a life event, one which is more severe than you'd expect. Anxiety Care UK describes it below:

An Adjustment Disorder occurs when the normal process of adaptation to one or more stressful life experiences is disrupted, and will occur within three months of the onset of this stressor or stressors. These stressors may be perceived as good or bad. AD is not the same as PTSD (post-traumatic stress disorder) which is usually a response to a much more severe stressor.

I had struggled to open up to my care coordinator because it just felt like she didn't care (ironic, considering her job title.) It seemed that I was just a burden to her. Before she'd gone off sick she'd told me she'd arrange an appointment with the outpatient team so I could get the medication sorted out. And yet, I received no correspondence from them whatsoever.

I rang the Community Mental Health Team, where Lauren worked, asking what I should do as I had no ongoing support or medication. Would someone else see me while she was off?

'What's your name?' the person on the phone asked.

'Ruth Fox.'

'Address?'

I read out my address.

'Bedfordshire?'

'Yes, I've just had to leave university and come back home,' I told them.

'Well, if that's the case then I'm afraid we can no longer support you. This is the Hertfordshire Community Mental Health Team. We have different NHS funds, so you'll have to go back to your GP in Bedfordshire.'

I had gone from acute care in hospital to absolutely nothing within the space of a few days. I couldn't even use the crisis numbers that had been made available to me in hospital due to my location. I had only moved 20 miles down the A1, but it made all the difference. The fact that it wasn't even my decision to leave university made this even more disheartening.

I didn't have the energy to see my GP again, because I knew that it meant telling my whole story again, being put on another referral list or trying a new – potentially unsuccessful – medication. I was done with all of it, to be honest. I was tired of being let down and never feeling cared for or loved. I was done with receiving no help from those who were supposed to provide it.

Every day I just hung on. I couldn't see beyond the next hour, let alone the next day. The nights were incredibly dark. I cut my wrists so many times and often slept in a bed wet with my own blood. I enjoyed the pain; it distracted me from my thoughts. I cut myself in the bath in the hope that it would end my life and I would no longer have to suffer. Luckily, I never did it deep enough. It was all so horrific, and still a vivid nightmare in my head even now. I was so confused. I tried to hang myself one night but didn't get very far. The pain was unbearable. I've never talked about that before. I'm still not sure if I was using self-harm as a release or means to end my life. It was bad.

My parents and sister had no idea what I was going through. I completely isolated myself and lost contact with the world. I was just an empty shell, an object with no real feeling, desire, or purpose. I woke up every morning despising the world and everything in it. Whenever I had to interact with anyone I had to put on a brave face, so I chose to completely withdraw myself.

There was nothing left in me with which I could keep fighting.

One evening, at the lowest point I'd ever reached, I planned my suicide and wrote my final letter. I've included it below, because without it I can pretend that it wasn't real.

It was so real.

Hello,

Clearly this is the hardest thing I've ever had to write. It saddens me greatly that it has come to this. But no matter how strong someone is, there is only so much they can take. The past few days I have felt very distant and as though I am looking down on my life, not living it, which is a horrendous way to live. All I need right now is peace and this is the only way I can achieve it.

Words cannot describe how difficult it has been and I just don't see a way out at all. There is nothing I look forward to and I have lost everything. I don't think people realise just how hard I am fighting, day in and day out. Every minute of every hour. I cry for no apparent reason and have had dozens of sleepless nights. It's exhausting and debilitating, and I just can't do it anymore.

Yes I had potential, drive, and ambition. But there is ultimately no point if I am being held back. I'm fed up of chasing people and being let down, and that is why professional help is no longer an option. When you're in a bad place and no one checks up on you or calls you when they say they are going to, when you're not offered any therapy or medication, there is no way of seeing anything getting better.

All I ask is that you try to help other young people and adults in similarly dark places. There are warning signs, but they can easily go unnoticed. I also ask that you remember me as the enthusiastic, chirpy, and cheeky girl before her life was engulfed by this horrific illness.

I thought I was going places, but when you can't even see beyond the next day it's hard to see how anything could be achieved.

So, my story has been cut short. I didn't become a pro footballer or anything. The darkness has swallowed that up.

Thank you and sorry. I know how selfish this is and the guilt has been burdening me for a while, but genuinely I see no other way out.

Keep strong and I'm sorry I can't be there on your journey, but I will always be by your side from above.

Sorry for everything.

All the love in the world,

Ruthie xxx

I planned how I would take my own life. I would get up before anyone else and walk to the field right next to the railway line that had several crossings with no lights. I would throw myself in front of a train. That's how I would end it. I replayed the act over and over again in my head that night. It was the last thing I thought about before falling into a confused and disrupted sleep.

My first thought the following morning was one of relief. Today was the day I could escape from my demons, the day when I could be completely at peace, when I could stop worrying the people around me. They sometimes talk about the high people experience before taking their own life. I've read about people being confused because, in the last moments before death, their loved ones look so relaxed and content. It's weird to be writing this, because I've had that feeling. It's a feeling of being at ease.

I laid in bed for hours and hours, knowing that as soon as I got up, I would do nothing but carry out the deed. I guess I was prolonging the last few moments I had left of my life ...

Suddenly I was startled to attention by a knock on my bedroom door.

'We're just going for coffee, Ruth,' my mum called out to me. 'Would you like to come?'

How oblivious my parents were. It wasn't their fault. They were moments away from losing their youngest daughter. It was sad that they didn't know how much pain I was in, but it was my fault for not opening up to them.

I think this distraction was all that I needed. I didn't go out with them, but my parents brought me back a takeaway coffee. This could have been the ideal time to take my life, but instead I thought about my mum's words. I was loved, I was cared about. One thing that has always been a factor for me when thinking about suicide is that, if I were to take my life, it would cause my family members to fall into the dark hole of depression. This is something I would never wish on anyone.

I sat in my bed, drinking the coffee slowly, appreciating and enjoying the taste. It really made me think of all the little things that made life worth living.

I didn't go to the field that day. I didn't leave the letter and I didn't take my own life. It was quite simply the scariest day of my life, one that I will never forget. I was scared to die, but life still scared me even more than that. Recovery seemed impossible and I didn't see a way out of that dark and infinite tunnel.

CHAPTER 15

LET SOMEONE KNOW

It took weeks for me to recover from that moment, to get to a stable place where I could start to look beyond the next minute, the next hour, and the next day. Eventually I got to a place where depression and suicidal thoughts were not the overriding aspects of my life. I could spend my days being more productive, rather than staying in my room.

I truly thought I was going to take my own life that day, and that was an emotional trauma which was hard to overcome, it still is. Those around me still had no idea of how dark things got.

It took me five weeks to drum up the courage to call up my doctor. She was unable to see me in person on that day because she didn't have any vacant appointments. But this was an emergency. Instead, I spoke to a doctor on duty over the phone and had to explain to her my whole history. The hospital had not sent my discharge letter to my doctor, so they had no knowledge of my being a patient there. Another miscommunication, another let down.

I was bloody fed up of saying the same stuff over and over again just because of the lack of communication between services. It exhausted me, but I had no other option but to put my trust in the system that had failed me repeatedly.

The doctor listened intently and was genuinely shocked that all this had happened without them knowing. She prescribed me venlafaxine, an antidepressant, and I started it that day. I was also told that the mental health specialist from the surgery would contact me about some therapy. Of course this never happened.

I recently took myself off medication in March because I'd had no reviews. They couldn't be bothered to check up on me, so quite frankly I found myself giving up on them as it felt like they had on me. I'd love to say that I took a pill, received some life-changing therapy, or reached a light bulb moment in my life.

But I would be lying. I didn't find a miraculous cure for depression, and I'm not claiming I did.

But I did get through.

Talking to people has helped me no end in my suffering and my recovery. People like Mr Donoghue continue to offer me an ear if I need it, which just relieves a little bit of the burden I'm carrying. Acceptance is another key part of my journey – acceptance of the fact that I don't have any A Levels, that uni didn't work out, that I was having a bad day. Accepting where you are at any one point is pivotal.

My advice is this: if you can talk to somebody – it doesn't matter who it is – about what is going on in your head, it means someone else has an idea of what you're going through. Telling them what you're worried about and what makes you angry helps you get it off your chest. It does offer comfort and reassurance.

I keep talking to people. If I have a bad day, I let someone know.

CHAPTER 16

LACK OF PROFESSIONAL HELP

I have a real issue with talking to mental health professionals. I truly recognise that there are some great professionals out there – in fact, most are probably amazing. I've had the pleasure of meeting some of them recently through my mental health advocacy work.

But unfortunately for me, in my greatest times of need, I was let down. Big time. It's understandable that people make mistakes, but for me it was just relentless. Below I have listed the mistakes that have led to my difficulty in trusting professionals.

I fully understand that the mental health services in this country are incredibly stretched, under-funded, and under-staffed. But I was let down to the point where it nearly cost me my life. Perhaps if I had just experienced one or two of these things instead of all of them, I would still have some continued faith in them. But this happened to me over and over again, not just on days when I was having an off day, but also when ending my life seemed like the only option.

- **My initial waiting time of six months to see CAMHS when I was 14.**

  Although I appreciate that this is a relatively short amount of time compared to a lot of others, I truly believe that if we'd explored my triggers and developed some coping mechanisms as soon as my issues arose, then perhaps I would not have relapsed so badly three years later. I was only offered CBT once I was in a better place myself, having been on medication. I imagine this happens to lots of people; they're referred for therapy, put on a long waiting list, given medication in the interim, medication helps, therapy appointment comes around, they don't want it because they feel well. To me, this reiterates that the system is flawed.

- **When I relapsed at 17, I was once again put on a long waiting list for CAMHS.**

This time I had a nine-month wait, during which time things deteriorated for me. I began self-harming just four days after starting fluoxetine. When I went to A&E for self-harm, I was waiting for seven hours before being seen. People may not class this as a let-down, but in my opinion, when you're stressed, anxious, and overwhelmed, sitting in a jam-packed waiting room for half a day is incredibly difficult.

- **Despite still needing support when I turned 18, all my care was dropped.**

I received a letter in the post a few days after my birthday, with no phone call or correspondence after that. Despite seeing a crisis team just a few weeks before, I was without any help from any services – child or adult – and left entirely on my own. I've seen transitions from child to adult services being advertised in waiting rooms. It never happened for me. It doesn't happen to a third of young people.

- **The university's "wellbeing services" never got back in touch with me.**

At university I went to the doctor when I was starting to feel the black cloud enveloping my life once again. He prescribed me fluoxetine and said he'd contact the "wellbeing services". I saw a lady for an initial assessment, opening up to her entirely about self-harming. She told me she'd get one of her team to get back in touch with me as she was going on maternity leave. That never happened.

- **After an eight-hour-round trip to A&E, I was bluntly told that my overdose wouldn't have killed me anyway.**

  I left the hospital at 3.00am that morning with no referral to services and no advice (other than to give the bottle to my friend and take the daily dose at her flat – my idea, not theirs). The only other thing they suggested was to talk to a particular professional at the university who could help me with my mental health (I don't want to be any more specific than that, for identity reasons). They didn't arrange a meeting; once again, this was my responsibility. I emailed the person in question the following day and received no reply for several weeks. In that time, I wasn't attending lectures or football training, and was self-harming all over my body. It took three emails from the Head of Performance Sport, the university first team coach, and my lecturer to finally get a reply and a meeting arranged. As soon as I was done with this meeting I was taken to the Community Mental Health Team and a crisis team, who arranged to see me every day.

- **The crisis team left me waiting anxiously for hours.**

  On day one, the crisis team said they'd come between 10.00am and noon. I was waiting patiently downstairs at my house during these two hours, kindly asking my housemates to steer clear of the kitchen as I had a meeting with someone. I was on edge as noon came and went. I received a call at 12.09pm saying they were now coming between 3.00pm and 5.00pm. This may seem like a minor thing, but when you're in that state of mind – when you can barely get through the next minute – it is devastating.

- **I saw the crisis team for four days and had a different person every day.**

  For this reason, I couldn't build a relationship with any of them. Because of this lack of trust, I didn't disclose how I was actually feeling and just became more withdrawn every day. One day when I was talking to a member of the crisis team, I put my head on the table because I was crying. About five minutes later I lifted it to find myself entirely on my own. The person didn't tell me they were leaving.

- **No one from the crisis team could see me on Sunday.**

I was told that because fewer staff worked on a Sunday, they only attended "high priority" patients (whatever that meant), and I wasn't on that list. I was told that someone would call and check how I was doing instead, but no one called me. This was the night I almost jumped in front of a car.

- **I called an ambulance and no one came.**

When I felt like I was going to overdose, I asked for help. I called an ambulance, which took a lot of courage. They said they'd call me back within two hours. It ended up being six. Anything could've happened to me in that time – and in fact it very nearly did.

- **I wasn't given any one-to-one psychological support in hospital.**

We did group CBT and Dialectical Behaviour Therapy sessions alongside generic art therapy classes, games, walking, and cooking sessions. I think I needed more intensive treatment. When I overdosed, I was taken off my medication and they didn't replace it with anything else.

- **In hospital I was diagnosed with bipolar depression, a diagnosis that confuses me and one with which I don't really agree.**

The doctor was going to start me on quetiapine, a mood stabiliser and antipsychotic, to level out my apparently sporadic moods. But my discharge came too soon, and he handed this responsibility to the outpatient team. I think it's important to mention here how important meds are.

119

The wrong ones can also be detrimental. I appreciate that potentially it could have helped, but I have no way of knowing this.

- **When I was discharged from hospital, my university chose to defer my place until the following year because they "didn't have the resources to support me".**

This was a tough blow, as I'd returned to university to get my life back. I now know that they probably made the right decision, but after speaking to the university more recently about this, I was told that I "hadn't utilised the university wellbeing services" and also that they had "assumed the care from hospital or community mental health teams would continue".

It's fair enough that they were handing over responsibility to the professionals in the field. They obviously assumed that I'd have a support network back at home. I truly respect this, but ultimately I was left entirely on my own. They didn't check in on me.

- **My care coordinator was supposed to arrange an appointment with me within seven days of discharge.**

She didn't contact me until the eighth day, when she told me I'd missed my appointment earlier that day. I'd never been given one.

- **My hospital discharge letter included a diagnosis for adjustment disorder, something the doctor had never discussed with me in hospital.**

How on Earth was I supposed to even begin to try to help myself deal with this if I didn't know I had it? I didn't even know what it was! It said on it my medication would be handed to the outpatients team, which never happened. To add to this, a copy of my discharge letter never arrived with my GP.

- **The lady in charge of mental health at my local GP surgery never got in touch.**

    At the start of January 2018 I finally managed to call my doctor's surgery. The NHS is stretched and my heart sank as I was told, after being on hold for over an hour and waiting in a queue of 23 patients, that there were no appointments left. They told me that a duty doctor would call me later on in the day instead. I knew this was my last chance to get help before I gave up on them all, so I agreed. The duty doctor was a nice enough lady, but she had no idea that I'd been in hospital. So, once I'd explained my whole story once again, she prescribed me venlafaxine and told me that the lady in charge of mental health at the surgery would be in touch. She never did get in touch, and I was on this medication for two months before the prescription ran out.

Since then, I have been medication-free and I haven't worked with a mental health professional since.

I'd like to reiterate that I am not against professionals at all. That whole umbrella encompasses so many avenues of mental health support, and I know there are incredible people out there doing incredible things. But these are the reasons that I'm so reluctant to reach out again. I put up a brick wall because of the way I have been treated. It's hard to know if I'll ever talk to a professional on a patient level again. I hope I won't have to, but I very well might need to. Emotional wounds take a long time to heal.

I'm certain that a lot of the professionals in my life had very caring natures. I'm sure that they wanted the best for me. But they were restricted heavily by the resources made available to them.

I don't want others to feel the same way as I do. Perhaps if this kind of information is spread more widely – and if it paints a stark picture of the current failings in the system – we can help shine a light on what needs to be improved. Maybe then things can move forward.

I've gained so much personal insight and awareness by going through the hardest parts of my life alone. I didn't have antidepressants hiding my symptoms or a psychologist holding my hand, unpacking the emotional stresses in my life. I'm not against either of these options, and I am fully aware that they are the answer for so many people, but for me they weren't available at the times I needed them the most.

I hope that no one has to go through what I've been through. No one deserves to be let down when they are at their most vulnerable, especially when they are crying out for help and fully accepting that they need it. I aspire to make a difference to the mental health services in my lifetime, whether that be in the smallest way or on a bigger scale.

I have hopefully started making steps towards doing this. I think it's invaluable having mental health professionals and also Members of Parliament hearing the first-hand experiences of service users.

CHAPTER 17

YOUNG PEOPLE'S MENTAL HEALTH IN SCHOOLS

Personally, I think schools have such an important role in educating young people about the issues that could face them. They should be taught how to maintain positive mental health, how to seek help if they're struggling, and how to look out for a friend or family member who is going through a tough time.

I had never heard of mental illness before I suffered from it. I thought depression was the same as sadness. I thought everything to do with the word "mental" – including mental health – meant being locked away in an institutional hospital and chained to a bed. This wasn't through misunderstanding or ignorance, but purely through a lack of knowledge. During years of Personal, Social, Health and Economy (PSHE) sessions in my time at school, I'd never once been told about mental health. It shouldn't be the case that you're only made aware of an issue when you're going through it, but that was definitely the case for me.

Teachers also need to be in a more confident position to deal with students struggling with their mental health. During my first bout of depression in Year 9, I was told I had to be in school by law. I was told that keeping the structure of the school day would help me. I understand and respect that this approach might work for some, or even most, students. But for me, driving to school crying, sitting with the school nurse, who I didn't click with, crying, and driving home crying didn't do anything to help me at all. Using a one-size-fits-all approach doesn't work, because each student's situation is different and brings with it its own challenges.

In Sixth Form I was lucky enough to have Mr Donoghue and a lot of other teachers who provided me with the time, support, and care that I needed. But I'm certain some others won't have that. Rather than just palming the issue off to professionals and doing nothing else, teachers can just listen to students. That can mean just as much.

Sitting with Mr Donoghue over a cup of tea and unloading to him helped me more than any conversations with CAMHS support workers, the school nurse or even acute treatment in hospital. As a teacher, you have a unique relationship with a student, and it is likely that they will trust you more than others. Mr Donoghue went above and beyond what was expected of him as a biology teacher, and for what reason? Because he cared about me. Because he wanted to see me well again. Because I was a human being who needed support.

Including me, 10 people in my year were struggling with depression during Year 13. I came out of Year 13 with no A Levels. Despite being an A-grade student throughout my whole time at school, playing first team hockey, rounders and football, and being a senior monitor and deputy house captain, I had no piece of paper with three letters on it to prove how academically able I was.

I'm not ashamed of that now, though. My school supported me emotionally during one of the hardest periods of my life. I grew as a rounded person more than I ever would have with my head buried in a textbook. I think I'd like to see, promoted within the education system, the message that grades, results, and qualifications are not everything. I recognise that GCSEs, A Levels, BTECs and degrees are essential in acting as a stepping stone towards certain careers, but the pressure put on students is, at times, unbearable.

League tables for results add pressure to senior management staff in schools, and that filters down to teachers and subsequently students too. There's also an expectation for students to be involved in anything and everything. I used to say yes to any school event: cross-country, house music, house dance, badminton, charities committee, science club, Higher Project Qualification (HPQ), English club, house debating, university challenge ... the list goes on. These activities are pivotal for student development, but how do we learn to say no if we need to? I only ever said no when I was too unwell to deal with anything. We need to emphasise how important balance is, otherwise we run the risk of driving our students into the ground and pushing them to breaking point.

Learning needs to be enjoyable and we need to learn because we want to, not just to pass an exam. For me, A Levels were too orientated around that final exam. They were so fixated on exam question techniques. If you used an incorrect style of writing or didn't include particular buzz words or phrases, you wouldn't get enough marks to get a decent grade.

A perfect example of this is during my chemistry AS Level exam, in which I got an E at the end of Year 12. Throughout the whole year I'd been passing with flying colours and regularly getting an A or B in any tests we did. For the final exam at the end of the year, however, apparently I'd revised in the wrong way (i.e. I knew the stuff but I hadn't written it in the right way) so I didn't do particularly well. But in the real world, once school and university is out of the way, when is this ever applicable?

Exams are overrated, in my opinion. I'd rather have students achieving slightly lower grades with less pressure put on them if that meant that they'd be much more prepared for real life. I didn't finish my English A Level and I don't have a degree in creative writing. Yet here I am, writing this book. Isn't this proof that qualifications aren't everything? I hope so.

I want to make my teachers proud. They have given so much to me and inspired me a huge amount. And I believe I can do that without receiving a first from *that* Russell Group university or having that career. We should be looking to create well-rounded individuals who are ready to positively impact their society. We shouldn't just be looking for straight As.

Teachers' mental health is just as important as students' mental health. We need to support teachers so that they can offer all they can to their students while feeling as little stress and pressure as possible. When teachers have to take time off– whatever the reason – it can be disruptive for students who have to have a supply teacher or another teacher. Of course, it's absolutely okay for them to take time off, and I support teachers in doing so, but I think providing emotional support to both teachers and students would be pivotal. It would give both parties the utmost chance of reaching their full potential.

It's also vital to have more than one option when looking for support. As I've mentioned, I didn't get on with the school nurse who was in charge of the mental health stuff at my school. This made things tough, because when people like Mr Donoghue weren't available, I felt like I was left entirely on my own. We are not all able to get on with everyone, so I think that having just one allocated "Head of Mental Health" or similar within a school carries its own risks. A student might withdraw even more if they know that the only person they can speak to is someone with whom they have no rapport.

Therefore, all teachers need to have some understanding of mental health issues, no matter how busy their timetables are (I'll reiterate that I think Mr Donoghue is probably the busiest teacher in the school). They need the time to listen to their students and check in with them on a personal level, not just an academic one. A one-to-one conversation should come before any email. It could just save a life.

In the same way that football coaches need to treat their players as people above all else, teachers must treat their students like individuals.

The more time and energy we devote to talking about and addressing mental health in schools, the more equipped young people will be in dealing with the issues facing them in later life. I genuinely believe that we can prevent so many people suffering from mental illness in the future. This is not only advantageous for people's quality of life, but it's also good from a government and financial point of view. We have the potential to reduce the billions of pounds lost to the economy in taking time off work due to mental ill health.

Personally, I am currently driving up and down the country trying to share my story in as many schools as I can. Hopefully I can help at least one person to learn about mental health or perhaps I can give someone the confidence to reach out if they are struggling or the awareness to recognise when a fellow student, family member, or teacher is going through a rough time.

My reason for doing all of this is to fill a gap I feel is missing in the education system. I want to spread a message that I wish I'd heard during my time in school. I want to give a talk to the 13-year-old Ruth Fox. Perhaps if I'd been just a little more aware at this age, depression wouldn't have felt so stigmatised, lonely and confusing. I would tell my younger self that 'This is okay, you are strong, this doesn't make you any weaker or an outsider. You can get through this.'

I think it's invaluable for young people to hear first-hand experiences from someone of a similar age. And that's why I'm talking about mine. The feedback from students, teachers and parents has empowered me to just keep doing it.

CHAPTER 18

A SAFE SPACE

When I was diagnosed with depression, I struggled to deal with the day-to-day battle. I struggled to socialise, I lost a lot of weight and strength, and that's when I had to make the hardest decision of my life. I decided to quit the only sport I had ever truly connected with, the only place where I could fully feel myself and express myself.

It was particularly hard because it was the foundation of my bond with Dad. It was the only thing I thought I had a chance of succeeding at on an elite level, the thing that distinguished me from others, and the thing that made me who I am. When I stopped playing football I lost my entire identity. I was no longer the girl who plays football or "Fox in the Box". I was now a skinny girl who could run a decent 10K time (42 minutes), but for no real purpose.

As you know, I was first advised to start training in the gym to help with rehab for my back injury. I was told to keep my fitness up and to try to gain some of my strength back, having lost so much from restricting my food intake. Year 9 was the first year you were allowed to train in the gym at school and, with a flashy, state-of-the-art new fitness suite having just been installed, I was looking forward to making use of it. I certainly did that over the next four years!

I approached Lou, who was the strength and conditioning coach at the school, and explained to her my situation. We soon came up with a training plan.

Over the next two years, I really focused in on developing myself in the gym. It helped distract me from the fact that there was a big hole in my life where football used to be. At this point I was still stick thin. Lou was concerned when I was lifting the empty bar for both bench and squats because I was so weak. I persevered, though, and began to lift more and more incrementally with her guidance and support. I learnt how to improve my techniques for all the main lifts: bench press, squat, deadlift, cleans, and snatches. I was the only girl who bench pressed, and one of the only girls in the gym.

In order to gain weight so that I wasn't dangerously thin, Lou told me to eat as much as I could, to stuff my face with anything and everything. It was almost as though I just needed some validation that it was okay to eat certain foods – foods that I had previously thought of as prohibited.

Lou knew what I'd been through. She knew why I'd lost weight and the struggle I'd come through. She, however, never mentioned it to me, and later explained to me that she wanted the gym to be – and to remain – my safe place where I could escape from the world. Most importantly, I wanted it to be an escape from my head.

When I returned to football at the end of Year 11, I continued to train in the gym. My focus was to aid my performance on the pitch by doing specific strength, agility, and conditioning exercises. In Sixth Form, I began to train with one of my best friends, Sarah. I also started training with Julie Rogers, a Paralympian who had competed at London 2012 in sitting volleyball and at Rio 2016 as a T42 classification sprinter.

These were two athletes competing at elite levels, and they were at the very top of their respective games. I was nowhere near this level, but I got so much out of training alongside them.

I was pushed week in, week out. Although Sarah could squat a stupid amount more than me, and Julie could probably clean over my bodyweight, I always rose above them in any mental tests (anything against the clock, competing against one another, or pushing above and beyond our limits). I loved the challenge and was hungry for more of the same.

When I left school I still wanted to continue to train, and that's when I began to train with Steve Linger on an individual basis. We trained together at the D (short for dungeon, which is what he calls his gym). When I finally opened up to him about my depression, he treated me like no other. I was shy, introverted, and lacking in confidence in my own ability when I first starting training with him, but I soon found that the sessions were right up my street. I began to see physical progress and improvements in my technique.

Some days I couldn't go to the gym. Anxiety washed over me like a cold shower and I was left exhausted and unmotivated before I'd even got in the car, or left my bed some days. Although I imagine this must've been frustrating for him, Steve was always really understanding and supportive. During my incredibly dark moments at uni, I'd chat to him regularly about how I was feeling. I presume he felt out of his depth, but he never showed it. I just felt cared for and supported.

There was a point where it was getting slightly out of hand. I missed sessions every week and had completely lost my focus, so he had a stern but very fair word with me. He told me that he only wanted to train the best. It hurt to hear at the time, but upon reflection it inspired me to get in regularly and train at my best. I now train twice a week and aspire to be the top female athlete he works with.

One morning before a 7.00am session, I attempted to the best of my ability to bandage up my wrist because I'd self-harmed the night before. It was poorly done, though, and during my pretty intense workout it came undone with the sweat dripping down my arms, revealing the raw cuts on my wrist. Steve didn't make any comments about the cuts; he just encouraged me as I pushed myself, so I powered through. This acted as motivation for me to work harder, to fight back against my depression.

Training with Steve has given me a focus, a motivation, and a shove in the right direction. He believed in me when I didn't believe in myself. He has supported me and proved himself to be more than just a strength and conditioning coach. We've built a strong bond. We hone in on the mental strength I always knew I had and test it week in, week out.

I'm gonna be honest here, because that's what this book is all about. I still struggle with my eating. I find it very hard to say yes to a piece of cake without feeling guilty, and I still view myself as very fat in the mirror. But my diet is so much more stable now, and I see food as fuel for my performance as well as a social activity. Steve has helped me no end with that.

In my opinion, it's all about balance and the 80 / 20 approach (80 per cent of time eating healthily, and the other 20 per cent less healthily, but only for a treat) is a good one. I know that if I allow it to get on top of me, the obsessive mindset will come into play and I will either eat all or nothing. I'm a very black and white thinker.

When I'm on top of it, and generally in a good headspace too, I can deal with this just fine. Diet plays a huge part in performing well on the pitch, and that drives me to stay balanced and sensible in what I eat.

Whether you're a seasoned athlete, or a regular gym-goer, the gym can be a place of utter sanctity and peace. The D is my safe place away from the world, away from the hustle and bustle of daily life. It is a place where I can focus solely on improving myself. For *me*.

CHAPTER 19

ADVICE FOR PEOPLE STRUGGLING WITH THEIR MENTAL HEALTH

I'm not a professional and will never claim to be one, but I thought I'd at least try to help someone who may be going through a tough time. These pieces of advice are things that may have helped me or others around me.

As I've mentioned, there's no one-size-fits-all, and I don't believe there's an ultimate cure for depression, unfortunately. What works for me might not work for you. Here's what has helped me, and it includes some useful advice from my trusty Twitter followers:

1. Talk

Above all, the most impactful and beneficial thing in my journey has been talking. Speaking out takes a weight off your shoulders, and it means that someone else is in your corner fighting with you. Opening up will not burden the other person, nor will it make them think any differently of you. It will also not make you any less of a person. One thing I've learnt through experience is to not expect an answer or a solution from anyone. At school,

I probably spoke to a dozen teachers. I was searching for something, anything that would help me. But ultimately, I've found that having two or three people to turn to and lean on in times of need is enough.

If you're having a bad day, talk to someone you trust. Talking to Mr Donoghue on a daily basis saw me through my school career, which had a huge impact on my life. It was the first time I had opened up about how I was truly feeling. It was the first time I had ever felt truly listened to and I felt appreciated and cared for, but most of all I didn't feel judged.

Find your Mr Donoghue, someone who will fight in your corner during the dark times and lend an ear whenever you need one.

2. Find acceptance

I think this is one of the most important keys to recovery; it certainly was for me. Accepting how you are feeling and understanding where you are in any one day is pivotal in your journey to being content with who you are. It's okay to not do what you set out to do. It's okay to do nothing. It's okay, whoever you are, whatever you do. You are amazing and unique and special and loved. Be proud of who you are. Learn from your past, but don't live in it.

3. Go for a walk

I kind of hate putting this in my list, because it would've annoyed me if someone suggested it in my darkest times. But the reason I've added it is because it genuinely can ease your feelings. I'm not saying it will solve anything – unfortunately none of the things on this list will – but for me, taking some time out, doing some gentle exercise, and putting in my earphones removed me from the intensity of my dark thoughts.

If, however, going for a walk is too difficult, that's okay too. Sometimes doing anything at all is too hard, and I fully understand that. But there is something quite special about being at one with nature. We do it less and less now in this modern world when really we probably need to do it more.

4. Remember it's okay not to be okay

This is most certainly my most used phrase, and one that I could never reiterate enough. We are all human beings and we all have our pitfalls. None of us are perfect and never will be. Some of the most well-known and successful people on this planet – J K Rowling, Stormzy, Dame Kelly Holmes – have been through some really tough times themselves. To me, this shows we are all human. Tough times are what make you stronger in the long run. Even if you feel weak, powerless, and helpless now, you are actually getting stronger every single day. Having the mental strength to keep going, no matter how hard it gets and no matter how much life throws at you, is proof of your character. Adversity builds strength. Never forget that.

5. Take it day by day

Kevin told me this while I was in hospital. It's probably one of the most effective things I've done. I still don't look too far ahead. Taking it day by day means you're not overwhelmed by the uncertainty of the future, and you can still set small, manageable goals. Since November, when I nearly took my own life, I've taken things day by day. I think that's been one of the key steps I've made.

6. Don't be afraid to say no

I've always been a yes person. I always want to please everyone, to help everyone, and to fill everyone's cups, even if mine is empty. But there's one thing that Mr Donoghue has said to me several times, and which he continues to tell me: 'Put Ruth first.'

Sometimes you need someone to remind you to look after yourself first. I can't solve everyone's problems. I do my best, but I just can't help everyone. Lots of people have reached out to me over the last five months or so. I've been able to offer some of them an ear and reassure them that someone is listening.

I've managed to give advice or recommendations to others. But sometimes I've just had to say, 'Look, I'm not feeling too good myself.' That's hard, but okay.

I always think back to the oxygen masks on planes. You're told to put your mask on before your baby's. It goes against your natural instinct, but you have to put you first. Learn to take a step back and take time for yourself. You're number one.

And now for some insights from my amazing followers:

- 'I think the best advice is to know you're not alone. Sometimes your lowest lows can lead to your highest highs. You're a perfect example of that. Yes, there are still bad days but that's okay because you remember why ... they're a part of your story, they make you who you are today.' @309Kat

- 'There are people who want to listen.' @ChelseaYosten

- 'The best advice I ever got was, "Nothing is permanent, everything changes. The good times will come again, but you need to be here to see them." Essentially, this too shall pass.' @MsGlynn2014

- 'Just get to tomorrow.' @jdickie

- 'The more you run, the faster [your illness] will. Stop, take a breath, and say, "You won't beat me, I will manage you."' @Talkindave

- 'Ask, "What has happened to you?" As opposed to asking, "What's the matter?" or "What's wrong?" The latter can make a person feel as though they have done something and are defensive about it. The former allows a person space and time to think, share, and talk.' @RachelOrr

CHAPTER 20

GRASP HOLD OF THE GOOD DAYS

April 2018, I'd had a bad day. I had tried to get on with mundane tasks like walking the dog, but my mind was occupied with a million thoughts. I tried pushing them to the back of my head, as I did every day, but some days it was just that much harder to do.

I knew that football training that evening would be my way out, my release. It had proved to be so on countless occasions throughout my life. I also knew that I had to let someone know that I was struggling. I texted my coach, Kevin, asking him if we could have a chat at training, and as usual he responded with 'Of course, mate. No problem.'

I was exhausted and drained from the day. The weight of the world was on my shoulders, a feeling I knew all too well. But I still tried to be as bubbly and smiley as possible on the outside. It took a lot of effort to do this, but it was even more effort letting people in. I didn't want people to ask me questions and go over and over what I'd heard a million times before. I just wanted to feel well.

When I drove to training, I turned up the music deafeningly loud and tried to focus on the football game ahead. And when

I arrived, put my boots on, and started kicking a ball around with the girls, I could feel the tension slowly starting to leave my shoulders. I could relax into myself, and I remembered who I was.

We started with some ball work, focusing on decision making and quick thinking. It took a while to get the hang of it, but it really made me focus and stay engaged throughout. I enjoyed pushing myself. I enjoyed being out of breath and I enjoyed working harder than anyone else.

We did this for about 20 minutes before collecting the cones and getting a drink. This was when Kevin asked me if now was a good time to chat. I said yes, and we wandered to the other side of the Astro for some space. We spoke for a while, about how I'd struggled to get professional help for my mental health issues, even though this was the avenue down which everyone wanted to push me.

'I feel like I'm being backed into a corner, or like I'm in some kind of limbo,' I explained. 'I know I need to make that step and contact a professional again. But I just can't because I've been let down too many times. I have nothing left to give.'

He listened. 'You don't have to do anything you don't want to do,' Kevin told me. 'You need to put yourself first. Perhaps you should meet up with your sister for a coffee? Tell her you miss her?'

I stared down at the floor. There was a lump in my throat. It was the first time, really, that someone had brought this up. Nothing had changed – I still felt that loss, still craved my sister's presence every single day of my life. I always felt that people would just tell me to get over it, especially as it was four years since she had left for university. But her leaving home had been a serious trauma for me. I knew we couldn't ever claw back that bond we'd had. It couldn't be replaced. I knew that, and it upset me.

Besides, I still had other issues. There was a lot of responsibility on my shoulders. My doctor still had no idea that I'd even been in hospital and now it was my job to fill her in. I also had to tell him about my suicide letter and the plan to take my own life. I was fighting a failing system, one that had let me down time after time, and now I was expected to just forget all of that and ring up my GP for an appointment. It frustrated the hell out of me.

'It's hard to fight a battle inside your head every single day,' I told Kevin, crouching down to the floor. Kevin crouched to my level. I felt supported and cared for, but at the same time I knew neither of them had the answers. No one does. I looked up, and through my tears I watched my teammates playing in front of me. I wanted to scream, I wanted to run away, I wanted to get in my car and drive for miles and miles ...

But I also wanted to be in the thick of it, tearing up the field.

I dried my eyes and composed myself. It was time to join in with the session again.

I knew I looked a mess, but I also knew that as soon as I was on that ball, I wouldn't care anymore. I wandered over and stood by another coach who high-fived me, chucked me a bib, and briefly explained the practice. I got it.

Before I touched the ball, I felt fragile and vulnerable. But as soon as it was at my feet, I was at home.

I launched myself in front of a striker who shot several times. I blocked three shots in a row. I had a deep-rooted determination to not concede a goal – the same level of determination I had to use every single day just to keep going. I received the ball on the back foot and pinged it wide, finding an outside player with a beautifully lofted pass. When the coach called out that the next goal wins, I dug deep. The desire to win always makes me dig deep. I swung in a cross from a wide position – just out of reach from the keeper and just behind the full-back – into the path of an oncoming striker who hit it home.

I loved this game.

We moved into a full-sized match where I took up my usual position as centre midfield. I demanded the ball wherever I was on the pitch. I demanded it from the keeper in order to start the build-up, from a winger to switch the play, and from the striker to set it back. I just loved the feeling of having a ball at my feet.

I could feel the smile creeping across my face as I acted as the pivot player. I received the ball from the left, passing it right, and then back out again to the left. This was a move we had been perfecting in training recently. I tried a skill where I allowed the ball to pass through my legs. I was hoping to nutmeg a teammate in the process, but it didn't pay off. I lost possession and sprinted back to try and regain it. I liked the freedom to be able to try these things out in training.

A corner came in and I lost my marker. I side-volley kicked the ball just wide of the right post.

'Who's going to take responsibility for that?' Kevin yelled as I jogged back. 'Who was supposed to be marking Ruth?'

I felt slightly smug.

After conceding a goal we kicked off again and the ball was played back to me. I took a touch, looked up, and swung a pinpoint-perfect pass to the right winger. With one touch they crossed the ball in for a striker to score. It was a cool finish.

It meant a lot to me to have teammates say well done after a good pass or move. I'm sure they'd seen me in a bit of state earlier on, so that extra encouragement spurred me on. My depression didn't stop me from being a footballer. Here it didn't define me in any way. I was reminded of that daily. I thrived when coaches pulled me back to talk me through a passage of play I had just been involved in; I loved it when they told me what I could have done better, what other options there had been.

I was hungry to learn, progress, and develop.

When the session came to an end I was gutted. I knew that my demons hadn't gone anywhere. They were there, ready to gnaw at my head for a few more hours that night. But at least I'd had an escape from them, for just a little while. I knew that whatever was going on in my personal life, football was always there for me.

Did I have urges to self-harm that day? No. Did I feel remotely suicidal? No. It was just a bad day. That happens frequently when you suffer from depression (and it happens to everyone to be honest.) The key is learning how to deal with bad days, and accepting fully that they are part of the recovery process.

Talking to someone about how you're feeling and trying to engage in your hobbies is vitally important. Chronic depression doesn't have a cure – we all wish it did, but the harsh reality is that it doesn't. It's more about finding coping mechanisms, managing, and dealing with the bad days. This is something I am still learning.

Oh, and grasping hold of the good ones ...

CHAPTER 21

THE BEAUTIFUL GAME

For me, football has been the only escape during the darkest moments of my life. There were days when I couldn't do it, but there were also days when that's all I could do. That mental image of playing football at the highest level, with crowds cheering me on, is what kept me occupied and kept my mind away from thoughts of suicide. I love to picture myself signing a shirt for a kid, being on live TV, having confidence on the ball, scoring goals, and crunching tackles.

I wanted to reach that level, no matter how much emotional pain I was in. Football provided me with the will to keep going so that I could improve as a player. If I killed myself, I couldn't do that. In this sense, football saved my life.

Often all I had was a tiny voice in the back of my head which said, *just keep going.* It's a voice that we all have; it's the one that tells you that you will finish these sprints, you will finish this last set in the gym, you will get through the next minute. That voice has been continually tested in my life, but it always wins. I always just keep going.

As human beings, we have a survival instinct to fight to be the fittest, the strongest, the quickest, and the best. That deep desire can push you through. I believe that on some level, a competitive nature is ingrained within all of us. How far are you willing to go before you quit?

Competing against opposition is easy. Competing against yourself is the true test. Sport offers us the chance to channel our natural competitiveness. We can push our bodies and our minds to the very limit of their capabilities. We can achieve things we never thought we could, and that increases self-belief, self-esteem, and confidence.

Sport has the ability to change an individual's situation. I've always been a different person on the pitch than I am in real life. I am a leader on the pitch, a play-maker. I am full of self-confidence, I am aggressive, and I want to win. This couldn't contrast more with the withdrawn, depressed person I was without it.

Football adds to who I am as a person. When all else is lost and it feels like everything has been taken away from me, football remains loyal. In itself it can be painful; it can beat you down to the ground, especially if you're not selected or playing many minutes despite giving it your all. But the positives of football far outweigh the negatives for me.

The football family is one that expands way beyond the club you play for. It spans the country – the world, in fact. We all have a shared love for the beautiful game. It is a sport which has the ability to both change and save lives.

CHAPTER 22

FOOTBALL'S RESPONSIBILITY IN MENTAL HEALTH

On a national basis I believe we're really behind in the development of understanding, support, and awareness of mental health in the football world. Football culture has been male-dominated for years and years. We have only recently been accepting women as professional players, coaches, referees, and fans.

We are all becoming observant of the facts surrounding male suicide. Suicide is the biggest killer of men under the age of 50. You're three to four times more likely to take your own life if you are a man. And 84 men take their lives in the UK alone every week – that's 12 every day, one every two hours. Those are horrifying statistics.

Due to the sheer number of men who watch and play football – as well as volunteering, coaching, refereeing, and chairing – the sport has a huge responsibility, in my eyes, to act as a platform to encourage people to speak out about how they feel.

The "macho" nature of the culture means that showing any sign of weakness is totally unacceptable. But one message that I will always try to promote is that it takes more strength to accept that you are struggling – and to ask for help – than to pretend everything is okay.

Here's a message for men in particular: it's okay to cry. It's okay to lose your job, or be broke, or find something difficult. It's okay to take a break. You have every right to go on medication for your mental health, just as you are for your physical health. The strongest men I know have been through so much but are open with what they have been through. Depression affects anyone and everyone. Counsellors and support groups are not just for women.

Some men may have other ways of expressing their emotions. They might not cry (or they might); they might not cut their wrists (or they might); they might not call a friend (or they might). But sometimes men turn to drink instead (is it coincidental that watching football is a very alcohol-orientated activity? I think not). Sometimes they punch walls, punch people, sleep around, gamble or withdraw from others. We might not associate these "laddish" activities with someone who is struggling, but in fact they could be expressions of a deeper emotion.

Football clubs are often hubs in the community. They're a coming together of friends, family, and even strangers – all there to watch the beautiful game. In my opinion, more needs to be done up and down the country to use the resources we have within clubs. We should use the magnitude of people involved in football to really push to raise awareness of mental health, whether that be through community trusts (much like Cambridge United's), mental health groups, helplines for players, or conversations between managers and the players. Player welfare should be of vital importance, from grassroots level up to the level of international football. Football would really benefit from more emotional support for those who need it, regardless of the level of play they're involved in.

As a player myself, I've had first-hand experience of the support available for players who are struggling with their mental health. The Player Football Association (PFA) offers counselling and support to players at a high level, but that only includes the top tier in women's football. When I first opened up at my club about my ongoing struggles with depression, I was told there was a chaplain I could speak to ...

Firstly, I'm not religious. Secondly, there's very little they could have done even if I was. Chaplains are not trained mental health professionals. I was frustrated that this was the only option available to me in seeking support within the club. Bearing in mind that the men's team is fully professional, I thought there would be some support in place for both the men's and women's teams to utilise. I resorted to just opening up to my coaches throughout the season, and obviously seeking external professional help, although this proved to be useless.

I'm fully aware now that I sometimes put them in very difficult positions. When you hear one of your players tell you they don't feel safe, or that they "can't do this anymore", what do you do? I was really lucky and grateful to have Kevin, Sean, and Alex, who handled it all very well. At times, when I refused to get help from a professional, I was told that my parents would be contacted. I couldn't think of anything worse. If I thought talking to my parents would help, I would've done it months before, but I knew all it would do was worry them, and that they would be unable to help. I found this really unfair. I was 18 years old, so there was no requirement by law to contact my parents. However, the duty of care to ensure that I was safe was also important. This puts people in a difficult position. I was mentally unstable and angry. It felt like I was being pushed further and further into a corner, and I did feel isolated.

In my opinion, all coaches should be mental health first aid trained, or at least have a module on mental health in their Level 1 coaching course. There is a module on physical first aid, so why not mental health first aid? I aspire to make this happen. I've helped to encourage 10 coaches at Cambridge United to be mental health first aid trainers which, I hope, is just a stepping stone in the bigger picture. I want other clubs and the FA as a whole to follow suit!

A player who is mentally unwell is vulnerable. They could be unsafe, in a far more dangerous way than if they had a graze or twisted ankle. As a manager or coach, you have a duty of care. You need to be able to deal with someone opening up to you about mental illness, suicidal thoughts, and self-harm. In safeguarding courses – also in the Level 1 course – you learn about how to respond to players disclosing information about physical or emotional abuse or neglect. You're even taught how to look out for the signs. And yet coaches are given no education on how to deal with mental ill health disclosure. In my opinion this is wrong on many levels, as these other safeguarding issues could lead to mental health issues (or vice-versa in some situations) anyway.

So many people panic as soon as they hear about tricky things like suicide and self-harm. We need to have the confidence to be able to ask the right questions:

'Do you feel suicidal?'

'Have you made a plan?'

A common misconception is that asking someone about suicide will put the idea in their head. This is definitely not the case. I was really privileged recently to appear on BBC Cambridgeshire Radio with two members of Cambridgeshire, Peterborough and South Lincolnshire (CPSL) MIND, who had just launched their STOP Suicide campaign. They were asking people to sign a pledge saying that they would openly ask about suicide. They are certain that openly talking about suicide will save lives, and I wholeheartedly agree. Over 70 per cent of people who die from suicide every year haven't been in touch with mental health services. It is our responsibility therefore, as members of the public, to spot signs of someone who is suicidal. We should be brave enough to ask the question, to ensure that an individual is safe, and get professional help if needed. As was reiterated in the Applied Suicide Intervention Skills Training (ASIST) course (which I recently completed), one conversation can literally save a life.

If a footballer has a physical injury, we give them sympathy. We send them a card in hospital if they've broken their leg. We wish them well in their recovery and rehab. Well, what should we do if they're in hospital for their mental health, as I was in November? I think I had two messages from teammates when I was in hospital and no visits.

Mental health and physical health need to be in balance for a player to reach their full potential as both a player and a person.

I think having players such as Chris Kirkland, Leon McKenzie, Cedric Anselin, Chris Sutton, Billy Kee, Stan Collymore, and Clarke Carlisle (all of which I've had the pleasure of speaking to) opening up about their battles with mental illness is pivotal in raising awareness. And, of course, it is inspiring. So many kids grow up aspiring to be footballers, and these players are huge role models in their lives. Having footballers talking about how they have felt during their darkest times gives others the strength and confidence to do the same.

In 2017 we heard about Aaron Lennon, who was detained under Section 136 of the Mental Health Act and was taken to hospital for assessment. There was an outpouring of support for the winger. Hopefully this helped some people to realise that no one is immune to mental illness, and in fact athletes are fairly likely to suffer.

The pressure and expectation put on professional athletes can really weigh down on them. It can also be hard to deal with injuries, as they can stop you from doing the one thing which makes you you. You also don't get that adrenalin rush or endorphin rush without training, which can be detrimental to an athlete's mental health (as I found out the hard way).

Access to emotional support and help must be available, just as physical resources are. Top gym memberships, performance coaches, diet plans, sleep analysis machines, recovery pools, and training grounds are all available, but realistically, a mentally unwell athlete won't be able to perform – just as a physically unfit one won't be able to either. The right mindset has to be switched on, self-esteem high, and self-doubt low. Mental and physical health go hand in hand for footballers and for everyone.

I'm lucky enough to have been part of a club with mental health at its forefront. I first got involved with Cambridge United Community Trust in January 2018, when they wanted one of the women's players to be filmed for some mental health, resilience, and wellbeing sessions that were going to be delivered in local secondary schools across Cambridge. I jumped at the idea and enthusiastically put myself forward. The videos – also featuring men's first team players and a scholar – were used in a six-week course delivered in lessons in several schools. The lessons included topics such as the importance of talking and listening, signs of mental ill health, stress, and the impact of social media on mental health.

Once the films were all done and edited I asked Ben, the CEO of the Trust, if I could be more involved as I was really passionate about the mental health awareness project they were launching. I thought having a young person's insight and personal experiences would be invaluable in adding strength and relatability to the project. Since then, I've been able to offer my own ideas and opinions to the Trust on how to move forward with the mental health work they are doing. As well as organising three mental health awareness evenings, I was lucky enough to be a guest speaker at one of them too. It was the first time I had ever shared my story in front of an audience, and it was a really humbling experience.

At Cambridge United there is a common vision, a shared sense of belonging, and a real family feeling. The senior management staff, who I am lucky enough to have spoken to, have players' welfare and emotional wellbeing at the top of their priorities. Results come second – the first priority is each individual player's improvement and potential. Mark Bonner, the assistant head coach, promises that 'The club will continue to do what it can to improve in its knowledge, understanding, and education in mental health.'

As a club they really are doing all they can to destigmatise mental health and encourage a society where it is fully accepted to talk about how we feel. I hope that other clubs can follow suit, and show that it really is okay not to be okay within the football community.

Mental and physical health can stand side by side. Within this beautiful game, we can ensure that everybody has the ability to reach their full potential and positively impact the lives of those around them.

CHAPTER 23

SPORT AS A LIFELINE: HOW SPORT HAS THE CAPACITY TO HELP ANY INDIVIDUAL

The sense of belonging within a team is immense and powerful. Whether you're playing five-a-side with work colleagues, going walking with a group of elderly friends, or representing Team GB in the Olympic Games, that unity and togetherness is absolutely second to none. It's fantastic to feel relaxed in the presence of those around you, to know that you all have a shared vision, outlook, and end goal. You are all in it together, through the good times and bad times. You never stand alone – and that's what makes sport so phenomenal.

Recently, while I was at the Cambridge United Community Trust gala dinner, I met a man called Steve Leys from Saffron Walden. He spoke about his son, Ronnie, a four-year-old with spastic diplegia (diplegic cerebral palsy). I asked Steve to write a little bit about Ronnie's story and the impact ambulant cerebral palsy sessions have on him. I hope you're inspired by his story as much as I was.

*

Belonging and Purpose: An essay by Steve Leys

Ronnie was born on 2nd April 2014, and we experienced many difficulties and overcame a lot of hurdles along the way. My wife Clare and I went from feeling excited about meeting Ronnie for the first time to being scared, worried, and panicked all within a few hours. If there was a way of truly explaining a rollercoaster of emotions, this was it.

Ronnie had suffered a brain haemorrhage during his ordeal. He then had a seizure on his first night – not the greatest welcome into this world. He spent the first 16 days of his life in the excellent care of Addenbrooke's Hospital and continued to show how determined he was to live. It was the start of what would be a very challenging life.

When leaving the hospital we asked the specialists to what extent Ronnie's brain damage would affect his life. We were told simply to take each day as it came and give Ronnie as much love as possible, because there was no clear indication of how badly Ronnie had been affected by this traumatic experience.

Our lowest point was when we were told, six days into Ronnie's life, that he had suffered brain damage. I can't tell you how painful and gut wrenching that news was for me and Clare. I remember going into an overly aggressive state of mind, wanting to hurt somebody or something. I just couldn't handle the news; it felt like I'd had my heart ripped out.

We didn't know what to do. Ronnie was still so helpless, and we just wanted to blame somebody.

Why him? we kept asking ourselves.

Ronnie was diagnosed with spastic diplegia cerebral palsy at age two. This is a type of cerebral palsy that affects both legs, and predominantly his right side. It has left him mildly deaf in his right ear, but we'd been warned about this. Despite all this, Ronnie continued to fight on. His self-belief and determination enabled him to do anything he wanted to do. Nothing held him back.

Ronnie was a late developer in terms of walking. He started at age two years and two months. At first it was very stop-start, as his legs just kept giving up on him. It was a massive blow to us all, but it was extremely tough for me to take, as a dad. I'd been making plans for Ronnie and his participation in football even while my wife Clare was carrying him during pregnancy – and that is no joke. What age could he start? What sessions were available to him? What team could he play for?

However, we wouldn't let the condition get in the way of this footballing dream.

Since then he has really gone from strength to strength. We came across the Cambridge United ambulant cerebral palsy football team through Ronnie's acting solicitors, Irwin Mitchell, who were fighting for compensation to help with his development going forward. We didn't get the compensation, because specialists suggested that Ronnie had caught a virus leading up to his birth, and therefore nothing could have been done to help our son. And yet he's now a keen sportsperson. He attends swimming, dance, and music lessons weekly, and he's a member of the aforementioned football team.

This is, without a doubt, his biggest passion. Playing football is one of the many reasons behind his incredible journey and progression to date.

The football sessions have helped us all massively, allowing us to find a release on a Saturday morning. Having spoken with other parents about their experiences and what they have done to help their children, we've exchanged stories and given advice to each other. The participants are nothing short of inspirational and give us all no excuses for not getting involved with sport. They are just incredible human beings who just want to play football.

There is a sense of belonging here for the children. After all their knockbacks – after all the doubt surrounding Ronnie's potential participation in sport – to see him and the others playing and running around with smiles on their faces gives us such pleasure. We love to see them celebrating scoring or savings goals. We watch them as they learn from misplaced passes or missed goals. They emulate their Premier League heroes.

These sessions mean that the children don't miss out on doing something that gives them so much pleasure and pride. Why should they miss out on physical activities just because they have been handed different cards in life?

There are not enough of these training sessions, and that in itself is a problem that needs solving.

Cambridge United has been superb in supporting the sessions. The players have been invited to a league game to have a kick about before kickoff. We've had Leon Legge and David Amoo involved with the training sessions. What a fantastic gesture. The kids still talk about it, and it gives them all a lift. It inspires them to work harder, and even, perhaps, to play for a league team one day.

Why not?

Steve Leys

*

One of my best friends from school is a top sprinter and rugby player. We used to train in the gym twice a week together and, although I was never competing in my sport at the same level as she was (she's represented England in several age groups in both touch rugby and contact rugby), we always trained with the same intensity and desire. I loved that. Here she shares her perspective on the impact sport has had on her life.

*

Distraction and Focus: An essay from Ruth's schoolmate

When I first started running and playing sport, it was only because I enjoyed it. Sport always made me feel good and it was something I could do relatively well. However, as I got older – especially within the last year – sport has become a bigger part of my life. I have come to depend on it.

The only time my brain is not overthinking or playing back painful memories is while I'm running or playing. I have begun to use sport as a tool to regulate my moods. It's what I look forward to every day. Whenever I have time off, my mood always plummets.

Playing sport gets me up in the morning. The challenge of playing well and organising my life around training up to seven times a week gives me a sense of purpose and a goal each day. My teammates always make me feel safe and at home, no matter how badly my day has gone. I know if I go to training I can escape my reality. I feel free of other pressures and stresses when I train.

Since undertaking my GCSEs I have used sport as a stress relief. It is my safe place. Training in the gym at school with Ruth was always one of my favourite things to do. It was my own little sanctuary. As I have got older the amount of time I need to spend training has increased exponentially in order to keep up with the increase of stresses and issues in my life. Sport has always had a hugely positive impact on me, but I worry that I am so dependent on it. One of my biggest fears is getting injured, as my coping mechanism will disappear.

Sarah Carter

CHAPTER 24

OUTSIDERS' PERSPECTIVES

BECKY, RUTH'S SISTER

This has been very difficult to write: I am not very articulate when it comes to sharing my feelings, as those close to me know. But I wanted to do this for Ruthie. I hope I can make you feel a fraction of the pride I feel for you.

Looking back on my childhood I see colour, sunshine, and laughter. As clichéd as it may seem, this is how I remember growing up with Ruthie. We were so different, but still the best of friends. Given any situation, we would find a way to make the other smile or cry with laughter. We were truly blessed. Ruthie excelled in life; she succeeded academically, on the football field, and philanthropically, filling those around her with joy. Every day I watched her grow into someone awe-inspiring. I thought Ruthie's light would always shine.

I was wrong. But I didn't even know how wrong I was. I had noticed something was going on with Ruth – the inexplicable bond of sisterhood made me aware. But hearing that Ruthie had been diagnosed with depression didn't feel real. The clinical accounts of depression in my university textbooks seemed inapplicable to the bright, strong young woman I knew and loved. It wasn't until I came home to visit that I realised the magnitude of her decline.

Seeing her like that felt as though her light had gone out. She'd lost her colour, her aspirations, her vitality. I saw in front of me a shadow of her former self, like the shed skin of a serpent. She looked cold and lifeless, her eyes dark and empty, her smile distant and futile. I could see the effort it took to act "normal". I knew she had succumbed to an unfathomable darkness beyond her resounding strength, and my parents were drained from the diagnosis too. They were doing all they could to help her. I didn't know what to do, and I felt increasingly resentful of my uselessness.

As time went on while I was miles away, it felt like I was on a vessel and my family were on a tiny raft, drifting further away, helplessly throwing aid at Ruthie who was drowning in a dark chasm of water. I wanted to be present; not overbearing or distant. Being at university meant I suffered a constant internal battle; I wanted to immerse myself in an essay or enjoy a night out with my flatmates. But then I would feel guilty, knowing that somewhere miles away Ruthie was alone in her room scrutinising her existence, while my parents persecuted themselves in the room next door. I despised the fact I could not be there to help any of them. I hated that she was on waiting lists to see psychiatrists when all I wanted to do was go to the hospital myself and push to the front of the queue.

All I could do was let her know I was there whenever she needed.

In November 2017, in the depths of winter, I received a text message from Ruth. She told me that she had been admitted to a Mental Health Unit as she had suffered from suicidal thoughts and overdosing. Not only this, but she had planned her suicide and written a note. She couldn't see any other way to escape her demons.

I was overwhelmed with emotion like I had never been before. Tears coursed down my hot cheeks. I was distraught. The thought of losing someone who meant so much to me turned my insides as cold as the callous winter night outside.

Anger surged through my veins. How could the mental health services let a young person down so drastically? Sorrow washed over me at the thought of her going through all that alone. I was sad for my mum and dad who had gone above and beyond to support.

I feel so blessed that we're a world away from that now. Ruthie is here today and what's more, she is thriving. She is stronger than ever and I am so proud. She is using her voice to help others and raising awareness about mental health.

Ruthie, you are amazing in every way. I could not be more proud to call you my sister. Keep doing you – I can't wait to see what the future has in store for you.

A COACH'S PERSPECTIVE: ALEX PULLING, RUTH'S COACH AT CAMBRIDGE UNITED WFC.

When you're part of a big coaching team with a big squad, you very rarely get one-on-one time with any player. But when you're observing, you always notice when players are or are not playing at the level you expect from them.

Despite Ruth's personal battles, she always seems to push herself to reach those levels. Football seems to give her a release on bad days. She's learnt to turn to the game when her anxiety builds up. During any training session she's always looking to be better, constantly questioning if she could do more. It was only when I began working with her one-on-one that I noticed she almost tries too hard. Then the coaching topics change from technical and tactical ability to the need to develop patience. Patience is something she can then transfer into her day-to-day life, when things don't go as planned or hoped.

Ruth's story shows that her resilience is developing daily. The smallest things used to break her, but now she can overcome obstacles and continue moving forward, even if it takes her a little bit longer than others.

There are times, during Ruth's darker moments, that you can't reply to some of her messages. It's not because you don't want to help – sometimes you just don't know what to say, and sometimes the right response could actually cause her greater stress. That's something I've had to learn, and a choice I have to stick to, based on what I believe.

From my point of view, Ruth has begun a completely new journey – one that will now lead her towards the life she wants and deserves. There may always be the odd day when she feels everything is going wrong, but she has learnt a lot and developed within such a short amount of time. She'll always be able to use her previous experiences to learn how to get through a tough time and continue on her path.

ADRIAN DURHAM, TALKSPORT BROADCASTER

Speaking from personal experience, it takes guts and faith and strength to come out and talk about depression. So for Ruth Fox to do it in her teenage years is remarkable. Seeing her pursue a life in which she helps others cope with the problems she faced alone surely makes even the most hard-boiled person wobble and fill up.

I am a voracious reader, so I downloaded Ruth's book and read it. Actually, I didn't read it. I soaked it in, every word of it. I got lost in the whole thing. When I read the suicide note I had to stop and take a moment to properly process exactly what this young footballer was going through before reading on. I then contacted Ruth to explain how I felt about her powerful story and why it meant so much to me, and, I'm sure, so many others.

Our shared experiences have led to a friendship and ongoing mutual support from which we've both benefitted.

The Ruth Fox you all see on Twitter or on TV isn't how Ruth is all the time. She's not putting on a front of course – she really is smart and confident. I was punching the air and cheering her on when I saw her live appearance on Sky Sports News! But she is also vulnerable, and needs help as she goes forward. We must all remember that.

Ruth's story is important, and I'm so proud of her for being brave enough to tell it. I thank her for putting her life on display so that she can help others.

I know she has certainly helped me.

ADAM WILLARD, RUTH'S PRIMARY SCHOOL PE TEACHER

I first met Ruth Fox in a lively Year 4 PE lesson in 2008. As I sat down to take the register I quickly realised the varying degrees of enthusiasm in terms of the children's attitudes towards sport and physical education. Ruth was sitting down on the carpet along with a group of children who clearly were excited at the prospect of a lesson in which they didn't have to sit down at a table. They seemed keen to learn through being active.

Ruth was a quietly confident child who always gave her best performance. She didn't feel the need to show off in front of others – that wasn't her style. She was very happy to be herself, even when that might appear to be uncool in others' eyes. She was one of the top children in the class for other subjects too, but more importantly to me she excelled in PE. She always took things in her stride and had the potential to be a leader and role model to others.

Ruth really stepped up and proved her talent to me in Year 5 when, for the first time, the school had a girl's football team. This year saw the birth of "Fox in the Box". She showed great will and tenacity when running around the pitch and hunting down the ball. She was always smiling as she went; you could clearly see that football made her happy.

Ruth always had a sporting intelligence. She knew when to be in the right place at the right time, and this was great for the team. Luckily for Ruth, the team was full of like-minded children who all wanted to learn. They enjoyed playing sport as much as she did.

In our first game against another local primary school, we won 9–1! I can remember how excited the girls were to represent their school with their parents cheering them on from the sidelines. In the game, Ruth scored five of our goals. I knew when Ruth had the ball in the box that she had the ability to score ... and she did! It was ever since that day that I called her "Fox in the Box".

After teaching Ruth for three years and seeing her and her fellow talented year group succeed in a range of sporting events, I have no doubt that her influence really helped them mature.

Finally the time came for Ruth to move on to a new school. She was more than ready for it. She had established friendships and learnt important social skills. Educationally, she was ready for the next step. And fortunately, Ruth went onto one of the best private schools in the area. Exciting times were ahead, and I was sure she would grab them with both hands and be a success.

I am sure that if you read this, you won't be able to marry it up with the word "depression". Why would a super talented, self-motivated young lady with a supportive family suffer with a mental health problem?

Well, the truth is that anyone is susceptible. Luckily for Ruth she has turned her so-called failures into successes, spreading the message that it's okay not to be okay.

Ruth, you are a success. Always fight like you did when you became "Fox in the Box".

CHAPTER 25

A RAY OF SUNSHINE

A chapter by Cathy Olphin, Ruth's classmate.

The funny thing about mental illness is that you can't always see that something is wrong. There are no broken bones or bandages, and symptoms don't show up on an x-ray. The symptoms are so varied and changeable that they are often unrecognisable or hidden away. No person or brain is the same – we all have unique experiences and thoughts which make us who we are.

For this reason, mental illness is complex and different in everyone you see. Sadly, there is no one-size-fits-all solution – all we can do is be a listening ear and a shoulder to lean on. I urge you all to have a conversation with your friends and listen as well as you can. Make sure that you are giving support to the people around you. Smile at them, because you never know what could be going through their minds.

I never knew that Ruth was ill, even when we were doing our GCSEs. I remember thinking that she'd become less talkative, but I simply put this down to exam stress. I thought it was a phase, and that seems to be the explanation used for most of the problems facing youth today. I noticed that she seemed thinner, but sadly that wasn't rare at all; students seemed to be constantly trying to diet and lose weight, even at a young age. Unexplained weight loss was almost the norm by this point. And, sadly, much of this behaviour is considered to be attention-seeking and vain, and so most students turn a blind eye to people's suffering. This highlights the crucial need for more education on mental illness and how to support those around us.

I definitely noticed when Ruth was suffering in our last year of A Levels, but not soon enough. Ruth is an incredible giggler – if she wasn't such a brilliant footballer she could definitely giggle for England! We'd always be cracking jokes in biology class, swapping puns with the teacher or asking for a cup of tea (often unsuccessfully). We have an arsenal of inside jokes that never fail to leave us in fits of laughter, and she really was (and still is) a ray of sunshine on those cold, early mornings.

After a while, I noticed that her giggling was beginning to sound forced. Her smile would fade as she turned away. One evening, I received a call and she was in floods of tears, asking me what the point of life was. It was at this point that I really became scared. I wasn't just scared for Ruth – I was scared of not having my ray of sunshine with me.

We all know the statistics. We hear that anyone can be affected by mental illness, and we all know someone who has been impacted by suicide. Despite this, I had never really believed that it would affect me, and I always believed that the people around me were too "strong" or "well off" to suffer from mental illness. How wrong I was.

The hardest thing about having a friend with mental illness is that you know them so well. Psychologists and doctors see a patient, whereas you see your best friend. You know their quirks, their sense of humour, and their weaknesses. Mental illness has the ability to change all of this. Things that used to make them passionate can leave them indifferent, and your sure-fire methods of making them laugh can stop working.

The most difficult thing for me was knowing when to leave Ruth alone – I wanted to find ways to help her and I didn't want to leave her to her thoughts. I'm a naturally very chirpy person, and I found it difficult to understand her lack of enthusiasm for the gossip I would tell her or the jokes I would make (although they were terrible). I couldn't even understand her lack of interest in her studies. We were conscientious high achievers and I couldn't imagine how she could no longer see any interest in the subjects we were learning.

I found it very difficult to get through to her, and I blamed myself for not doing a better job. Over time, I realised that the most important thing that you can do is just to listen without judgement. I let her know that I believe her and that I understand what she's going through. I realised that trying to find solutions was pointless, because it was up to her to become well again. All you can do is give unconditional love and support.

Ruth is truly the strongest person I know. She knew what she needed to do to get better and succeeded in finding a way to get through her mental illness. She knew the importance of sharing her thoughts and feelings and would let people know when things were getting worse so that she could have a support network around her. She was open about how she was feeling, which takes tremendous courage.

I could see how much it pained Ruth to see everyone else achieving things when she had to give up her studies. I knew she was frustrated at being left behind. I think this is why she made the last-minute decision to go to university. It was heartbreaking to see all her efforts and struggles seemingly coming to no avail, and it felt unfair that Ruth was being hindered through no fault of her own.

Luckily, Ruth isn't the kind to be beaten. She has proven that university and qualifications are not essential to achieving your goals. What is really required is passion and tenacity, and Ruth certainly has bucket-loads of that. She is now working around the country to help other people in her situation and achieving things other 19-year-olds could only dream of. I am so incredibly proud of her journey and recovery, and I know that thanks to speaking up about her struggles, she will make it easier for people to speak up in the future.

She really is a true hero.

CHAPTER 26

A SHINING LIGHT

A chapter by Ruth's friend, Becky Howe.

Ruth is the shining light in my life. Whenever we are together, I belly laugh so hard you'd think I'd have abs! But occasionally the light dims, and she needs the help and support of the people around her to get through some incredibly tough times.

When Ruth was first diagnosed with depression, we were in Year 9 at school. I remember coming home from school one day and saying to my mum, 'I don't think Ruth wants to be friends with me anymore.' Ruth and I were inseparable; where Ruth went, I went. But suddenly she became quiet, reserved, and didn't seem to want to talk to me. Her weight loss was perhaps a more visible symptom of the illness at this point. It was very visible, especially in her face. Some of our peers were quite mean, commenting about how she was "too thin". I can't imagine what Ruth was going through at this stage.

Behind this was a struggle that none of us knew about.

When Ruth felt comfortable telling me what she was going through, she sent me a very helpful video entitled *I Had a Black Dog. His Name was Depression.* I found this invaluable in trying to understand Ruth's feelings and behaviour, and I would recommend it to anyone who finds themselves in a similar situation to mine.

We found it much easier to talk about it over social media rather than face to face. This is a great tool, although it does have its drawbacks. You can't truly tell how someone is feeling when they're behind a screen. It also feels like you can do very little to help them.

Ruth is very strong willed and determined. She would tell me that she no longer wanted to go to counselling, or that she hated the school nurse, who wasn't often diplomatic with her words. She would say that her parents couldn't help, but actually we didn't really know what more they could do. I can't imagine how hard it must have been for them to suddenly see their bubbly, confident daughter knocked down by an invisible illness.

Often we disagreed on what was best for her to do. It took me a while to come to the conclusion that only Ruth could make herself better. I just had to be there to support her, rather than telling her what to do.

I felt selfish quite a lot, mainly because sometimes I just needed a break. I felt like it was my mission to make Ruth better. I wanted to find that one magic trick that would work. It takes a lot of emotional energy to constantly support someone. I often found myself taking on all her feelings and nearly crashing myself. I'd always be conscious about saying the right thing. I didn't want to trigger any bad thoughts or feelings. I needed reassurance that I was doing a good job and not being a hindrance.

These feelings came back again when Ruth's demons returned during our A Levels.

When the depression reared its ugly head again in 2017, I thought I knew what was coming. I knew we'd get through it, but I didn't expect it to be as challenging as it was. A particularly prominent memory for me is when Ruth sent me a picture of the cuts on her arms. This made me realise that she was in serious trouble and she needed professional help. I had a chat to Mr White, our Head of Sixth Form, about it. He told me not to talk to her on social media. This was a hard thing to do, but it probably benefitted us both for the little time we had left at school.

Most of our teachers were amazing during this time. Mr Donoghue, our biology teacher, was the first person that Ruth reached out to when the depression returned. He wasn't a health professional, and he certainly didn't tell Ruth what was wrong or right to do. He listened when Ruth needed him, and he would always check in with the both of us every few days.

I've cried many a time to both these teachers, which seems silly to say now. It seemed they understood what it felt like to be helpless in a situation.

I cry a lot, often about silly things like a dog on a video, or on the last day of school. However, the best time I cried was at the school Sports Awards. Ruth Fox, my best friend and role model, won a legacy award for her contribution to sport in the school, and I sat there next to a deputy head teacher bawling my eyes out. Ruth makes me immensely proud. She encourages me and makes me more determined to succeed every day.

At school, she challenged me academically and in sport. I wouldn't be the lover of sport that I am today if it wasn't for Ruth believing in me. On the dark days we'd go to the gym together – even if it was in silence. We joked that she was my personal trainer and I'd pay her in cups of tea. Oh, the laughs we have had!

I am going to be honest in Year 9 there were times when I thought Ruth was milking it or doing it for attention. I hadn't heard of depression before and I didn't know much about it. Thankfully, I now see how naïve I was. This is the opinion that is slowly changing, especially among the older generation. And it's thanks to the determination and perseverance of people like Ruth.

CHAPTER 27

MR DONOGHUE

A letter by Mr Donoghue, Ruth's teacher

I have finally got to sit down and give this a good read. Admittedly, it was my fourth attempt as I kept on getting pulled away.

Wow, what an amazing story to share ... as you said, if it inspires a single person, it would be worth it. Mr Bywater (Ruth's English teacher) and Mr Marsh have all told me how touched they were when hearing your story.

Mr Hall would have been genuinely proud of you that night at the Sports Awards. Just before he left he offered me words of wisdom when dealing with pastoral issues: he told me that he had lost a student to suicide while being a Head of Sixth Form in a previous school.

You have fought an epic journey. It's had its ups, its very deep downs and a few curves along the way. However, you have come out stronger than ever. You are even more determined to do right for yourself, and other people who are in your situation.

It has taken some courage to put all of this down on paper. People shy away from sharing even the most vague details of themselves, but you have laid it all out on the table.

Keep spreading the word and fighting your fight. You have inspired a number of people here at school and I hope that you can inspire so many others.

Thank you for also having me as part of your journey. You didn't have to talk to me, but you have helped me understand depression so much more. I will never be an expert as I may never walk in your shoes, but I can at least feel comforted by the fact that I have helped you with your battle. Hopefully I can help more people in the future.

Well done!

CHAPTER 28

NOW AND THE FUTURE

The only time you should look back is in seeing how far you've come.

I hope my story shows that with perseverance, determination, and the sheer willingness to keep going – or, sometimes, just "hanging on" – difficult times can come to an end. Doors can, and will, open to reveal a more positive and hopeful future. It seems only right that I share some of the opportunities that have come my way during my recovery.

Since self-publishing my eBook on Amazon in January 2018, there's been a continual upward trend in the amount of attention my story has garnered. I first posted about it on Twitter, and I decided to use this social media platform to try to spread my message and reach as many people as possible. Within the first four months of doing so, I'd gained more than 4,000 followers (you can find me @Foxinthebox05). My most unusual and high-profile follower is Neville Southall, the man who has made the most appearances for Everton and is Wales' most capped player. He is often referred to as the greatest goalkeeper of his generation. Neville reached out to me and told me how much my story touched him, and he has subsequently done a lot in raising awareness of mental health. He's reached some 143,000 people with each of his tweets. It's amazing to think that I was the catalyst for his passion for this.

I had the pleasure of meeting Nev in March 2018 at a Mental Health Football Association football tournament in Wales, which brought together people who were struggling with their mental health from all around the country to play football. I was also honoured to be made an ambassador of this amazing, completely volunteer-run organisation as a result of my campaigning, alongside big Nev.

I've featured on a variety of media platforms and I've been able to meet some amazing people along the way. Bearing in mind that I'd never been on the radio, had a camera in my face, been live on TV, or spoken in front of an audience before, I think it's safe to say I've had to adapt pretty quickly.

I've been live on BBC Cambridgeshire six times. I've been a guest on Cambridge 105 Radio and St Albans-based radio station, Verulam. Sharing my story on the radio was easier than I ever thought it would be. I'm incredibly passionate about this subject, and I firmly believe in it. That makes it so much easier. I don't think of the hundreds or thousands of people who could potentially be listening; I just think of the impact of my words. In fact, that is all I think about in my day-to-day life. If I can make an impact on just one person's life and give them a glimmer of hope (because that is sometimes all it takes), then it's 100% worth it. I want to help pull them out of that dark, dark place that I've found myself in, to make them know they are not alone, to make them more aware.

I've also done a few podcasts with people, the most enjoyable one being with Drewe Broughton, an ex-professional footballer. His honesty, integrity, and sheer strength is testament to him, and he's just an all-round good guy. He has been broken and battered by the beautiful game. He's struggled to find himself, to be at his best, to fit in. He's been left bankrupt, homeless, depressed, and without a family, but he's turned his bad experiences into something positive. Now he helps footballers emotionally.

I've learnt a huge amount from this man. He's shown me that vulnerability and sensitivity are not weaknesses. He's taught me that the footballer's gift is also a curse – the desire, the drive, the intensity, the ambition, the hunger has its pitfalls. Despite the 20 years between us, we connect on a level that I've never experienced with anyone else before. He just gets it.

The most incredible experience that's come off the back of sharing my story was the day spent filming with Alan Myers. Alan and his cameraman drove down from Liverpool to capture a day in my life, to be broadcast on *Sportswomen* on Sky Sports News. I was slightly taken aback that they wanted to film me; I'm genuinely nothing special. I'm just a girl with a story, a message, and a voice, but that seemed to be enough for them to make the 373 mile-round trip. They came to my house and we filmed the intimate and very open interview in my living room, followed by some casual shots of me making a cup of tea. (We had to re-shoot this about seven times. This simple, everyday task was somewhat more difficult with a £20,000 camera in my face.)

We also filmed a training session with Steve, heard his perspective on things, grabbed a cheeky Costa (hearing some great stories about Paul Gascoigne), and filmed a training session at Cambridge United too. It was literally one of the best days of my life, and it was pretty surreal seeing it broadcast to thousands and thousands of people.

That wasn't it in terms of my TV appearances, though ... I was lucky enough to be invited back by Sky Sports News to appear live on *Sportswomen* during Mental Health Awareness Week. Again, it was an incredible experience. I was able to be open about my story while offering advice for anyone out there who was watching and struggling. As I write this (yet again, in Costa), I am also halfway through filming a piece with BBC Look East. Part one features the cameraman sitting in on a meeting between me and my local MP, Alistair Burt (also Minister of State for the Middle East at the Foreign and Commonwealth Office, and the Minister of State at the Department for International Development). Here I share with him my experiences with the local mental health services and how I'd like to see them improved. Part two will be helping to deliver a mental health programme in a local school with Cambridge United Community Trust.

In February, following quite a lot of exposure for my story, a message popped up on my Twitter account from Trigger Publishing (the lovely lot who have published my book). They told me they'd be really interested in having my story published in paperback as part of their Inspirational Series. Following a meeting with Stephanie, my lovely editor, who I assumed would tell me, 'Sorry, Ruth, we've had a rethink and we don't think your story will be powerful / long / impactful enough,' I started to think about how I would go about expanding it. They were serious about publishing my book, and I was shocked.

I hadn't even finished my English A Levels, and now here I was, writing a book at just 19 years old. Life has a funny way of turning out.

Along with Neville Southall, I've also had the pleasure of meeting David Moyes (former Manchester United and Everton manager) at a gala dinner, during which he actually wanted to come and speak to me. He had heard about what I was doing and the message I was trying to spread. After years of watching this man on *Match of the Day*, it was crazy to speak in real life. He was a really down to earth and emotionally switched on man. I've also been lucky enough to meet Stan Collymore, Lee Dixon, and Mark Bright – three more footballing legends.

I've never done anything in my life for recognition. I've always been a "head down and get on with it" kind of person. So, for me, it's more than special to receive acknowledgement for my message, and for opening up about my most vulnerable times. I do it in the hope of helping others in a similar position to mine.

In March 2018 I was honoured to be named the Cambridge United Ethos Community Hero of the Day, which involved handing the match-day ball to the referee. I was also chosen to be the Community Volunteer of the Year. I was incredibly humbled to receive this award, particularly because I'd only been campaigning for just under five months. The fact that the club thought I was worthy of this award for the entire year was something incredibly special.

I think this finally made me believe that maybe I was doing something right. I had managed to turn my life around, holding on when life seemed so dark and futile. It was certainly starting to be worth all the pain.

One of my favourite things to do now is to talk to young people in schools. My reason for this? To give a talk I wish I'd had in my school career. If I'd been a little more aware in my early teens, perhaps I would have been better equipped to deal with the difficult years that followed. What I needed was to hear a real-life experience, an honest story, a story of hope.

I am passionate about helping young people because I have a true appreciation of how tough it is to grow up in this era. We have pressures from school and pressures from social media – the expectation, the comparisons, the likes, the judgement, the competition, the validity. I get it. And I really hope I can engage with the people I talk to and provoke an emotional connection, just like Mr Jenkins did with me some six years ago.

I go into every talk with the aim of impacting just one person. Perhaps they've struggled themselves, perhaps they are currently struggling; perhaps their mum is struggling, or perhaps a friend. Maybe they have no idea what mental illness is and how it can affect an individual. I aspire to promote positive mental health, offer advice, raise awareness and, most importantly, encourage people to talk.

In one of my more recent talks at a school in Stoke, I had a number of students approach me afterwards to open up about their own battles. One particular Year 8 girl sticks in my head, and I think she always will. She described, in an incredibly composed manner, the moment she had come home from school to find her dad lying in the bath with needles sticking out of his arm. He had taken his own life.

She had just come home from school, on a day just like any other. She was 11 years old. No child deserves find their parent like that. Not ever. I gave her a hug and told her she was incredibly strong. I could already tell she was going to be a huge inspiration. If I ever doubt what I'm doing or have a bad day, I picture her in my head, so composed and so brave. I feel empowered to do this for her and to stop others reaching her father's point of despair.

I also recently spoke at a teacher's conference in Newcastle in front of 100 educational professionals. I was chosen to be the keynote speaker. They all stuck with me: the response from that talk, the teacher who came up to me in tears afterwards, the incoming messages from days later, the handshakes at the end of the event, the #BeMoreLikeMrDonoghue hashtag that was trending on Twitter that evening, the applause that continued around me while I sat back down having finished speaking. It was in the hotel room that night that I had a lightbulb moment. I realised that this is something I need to do. This is my calling, my direction in life, and this is where I can make the most impact. I have never been a public speaker, but now I feel at home up there.

I have no idea what the long-term future holds for me, if I'm honest. That in itself is daunting and scary. I want to continue sharing my story and seeing where that takes me. In the long term I'd like to work with young people, whether that be through teaching and emulating some of my inspirational teachers, or in another way. I'm not quite sure. What I do know is that I'm never alone. I have an ever-growing support network around me, people who help guide me through this extraordinary thing called life. I still meet Mr Donoghue for a strong cup of Yorkshire tea and he still always on the end of an email for any advice or support I need.

Every day I aspire to reach my full potential in all that I do and impact as many people as I can. Regardless of which direction my life goes, these goals remain constant. And who knows? Maybe this book will need a sequel anyway ...

Thank you for taking the time to read my story. If I ask one thing of you, it is to check in on somebody today; an old friend, a colleague who has been quiet recently, a teammate who hasn't trained in a while. You never know what someone else is going through. One conversation could just save their life.

Ruth x

AFTERWORD

I first came into contact with Ruth when I approached Cambridge United Women's Football Club. I wanted to know whether any of their players would be willing to be involved with a mental health project at Cambridge United Community Trust – the charitable arm of Cambridge United Football Club. We were developing the project for secondary schools and hoped that some of the women's team would support the project by recording video interviews, which would be played during lessons. Ruth volunteered to be a part of this project and so came into the club to record an interview.

When I recorded with Ruth, it was clear that she was extremely passionate about the subject. She clearly hadn't just volunteered to be a part of the project for the sake of it. She answered the questions articulately and intensely. Ruth emphasised the importance of destigmatisation of mental health issues. She highlighted a vital message: it's okay to not be okay.

I was extremely surprised at how articulate and mature she was for an 18-year-old, especially since she was talking about a difficult issue to discuss.

Ruth's messages chimed very well with our project. We wanted to speak to secondary school children, mainly between the ages of 12 and 14, to educate them about their own mental health. We wanted to teach them where to seek help if they need it. They need to understand that everyone has mental health and that it needs to be looked after in a similar way to physical health. We hope to use the power of sport and the brand of our professional football club to break down assumptions about mental illness. This is a particularly powerful thing for an organisation such as a football club to do, because sport can often be seen as an arena that is averse to talking about feelings. Often in sport they're seen as weaknesses.

Since the time of her interview, Ruth has become increasingly active on social media. Subsequently she has appeared in print, on radio, and on television, publicising her story. Obviously it's culminated in the publication of this book. She has spoken out in a courageous manner about the problems she has been dealing with and encouraged other people to see hope where they might otherwise only see despair.

This is an extremely laudable thing to do and one that has undoubtedly helped many other people.

Indeed, I witnessed first-hand Ruth helping somebody. In March 2018 Cambridge United Community Trust held a mental health awareness evening surrounding the theme "Time to Talk". Ruth attended and gave one of her first public speeches at the event. Afterwards, a man in the audience put his hand up and told the room that he had travelled to Cambridge from London because he wanted to see and thank Ruth. Her openness on social media about her struggles had helped him realise that he wasn't alone in his depression, and therefore she had helped him move away from some of his suicidal thoughts.

Ruth's work in raising awareness of these important issues had clearly had a huge impact on this man's life.

The work of campaigners like Ruth is hugely valuable. It breaks down stigma and encourages individuals facing problems to speak up and seek help. But despite our progress, we still have a long way to go before mental health is put on an equal platform with physical health. There has been increasing rhetoric suggesting this will happen – partially fuelled by the Royals' Heads Together campaign in 2017 – but as of yet the serious money has not flowed into mental health services. Instead, charitable organisations and schools are left to deal with the issues, particularly for those at the less severe end of the spectrum and for adolescents.

Unfortunately, at the moment our society is not necessarily conducive to positive mental health. There are frequent media stories about the growing extent of poverty, cuts to disability benefits, and NHS problems. This is combined with the growing use of social media, which can promote unhealthy degrees of comparison between peers and celebrities alike. Indeed the high (and, over recent years, growing) levels of income inequality in the UK could also contribute to poor mental health. This argument is made in the ground-breaking book *The Spirit Level* by Wilkinson and Pickett.

Football has a potential role to play in solving this problem. We believe that by openly prioritising mental health and wellbeing, we can encourage people to understand the positive effects that looking after your own mental health – as well as the mental health of others around you – can have on your life.

We must all fight for good mental health. We must do this by understanding that society can contribute. We must support others who may be struggling. Nobody should be afraid or unable to seek support. Ruth's work is important in driving forward all of these agendas. I hope she, and others like her, are successful in their endeavours. We need all of them to be successful if we are to live in a happy society, because a happy society truly relies on the active promotion of positive mental health.

Ben Szreter, Cambridge United Community Trust

ACKNOWLEDGEMENTS

With thanks to Mum, Dad and Becky for your unconditional love and support in all that I do. Without you I wouldn't still be here to share my story.

For all the staff at school who supported me through one of the toughest years of my life. A special thanks to Mr White for reminding me that "health and happiness comes before education", a message I now try to spread myself. Also Mr Bywater, my English teacher, for always having faith in my writing ability and for showing me that you don't need an English A Level to write a book! I hope to make you all proud.

Thanks to all at Cambridge United FC for supporting me incredibly in my endeavours to raise awareness of mental health and for supporting me massively on a personal level.

With thanks to all those who have contributed to this book and to Stephanie for tying it all together.

For anyone who has lent me an ear or supported me in any way, shape or form and believed in me when I didn't believe in myself, thank you.

**If you found this book interesting ...
why not read these next?**

Barber Talk

Taking Pride in Men's Mental Health

What do you do if you lose a very close friend to suicide?
Encourage others to open up within a safe space. In *Barber
Talk,* Tom takes a tragedy and creates a positive mental health
movement, encouraging men to talk about their mental health
in barbershops all across the world.

Must Try Harder

Adventures in Anxiety

After 30 years hiding in the shadows, beset by extreme social anxiety, Paula McGuire decided to change her worldview - one terrifying and exhilarating challenge at a time. In this book, Paula shares her extraordinary journey from recluse to adventurer.

Today, Just Like Yesterday

Defying Dysthymia One Challenge at a Time

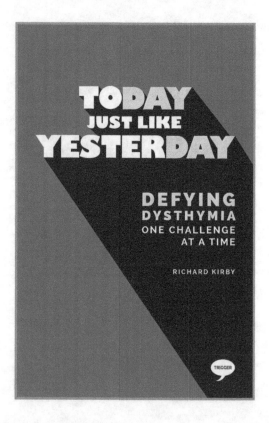

Today Just Like Yesterday tells the breathtaking story of Richard's experiences with depression and dysthymia. With this in mind, he set out over the next few years to undertake 100 mental, physical and emotional challenges designed to raise awareness of the condition.

the *Shaw* mind

FOUNDATION

Creating hope for children,
adults and families

Sign up to our charity, The Shaw Mind Foundation

www.shawmindfoundation.org

and keep in touch with us; we would love to hear
from you.

*We aim to end the suffering and despair caused by mental
health issues. Our goal is to make help and support available
for every single person in society, from all walks of life. We will
never stop offering hope. These are our promises.*